DADDY

IS THAT STORY

TRUE

OR

WERE YOU

JUST

PREACHING?

JAMES W. MOORE

Abingdon Press

NASHVILLE

DADDY, IS THAT STORY TRUE, OR WERE YOU JUST PREACHING?

This book is printed on acid-free paper.

Library of Congress Cataloging-in-Publication Data has been requested.

ISBN 978-1-4267-4463-1

Scripture quotations, unless otherwise noted, are from the New Revised Standard Version of the Bible, copyright 1989, Division of Christian Education of the National Council of the Churches of Christ in the United States of America. Used by permission. All rights reserved.

Scripture quotations marked KJV are from The Authorized (King James) Version. Rights in the Authorized Version in the United Kingdom are vested in the Crown. Reproduced by permission of the Crown's patentee, Cambridge University Press.

Scripture quotations marked Phillips are from *The New Testament in Modern English,* rev. ed., trans. J. B. Phillips.

12 13 14 15 16 17 18 19 20 21—10 9 8 7 6 5 4 3 2 1

MANUFACTURED IN THE UNITED STATES OF AMERICA

For all of the supportive members of my family

who have heard most of my stories

(some of the stories more than once)

and who have always listened

with focused attention and unconditional love.

You never cease to amaze me!

CONTENTS

Contents

Contents

Contents

✦✦✦✦✦✦✦✦✦✦✦✦✦✦✦✦✦✦✦✦✦✦✦✦✦✦✦✦✦✦✦✦

DADDY, IS THAT STORY TRUE, OR WERE YOU JUST PREACHING?

Daddy, is that story you told this morning true, or were you just preaching?" That was the sincere question that came from the little boy in the car seat in the back of our car as we drove home from church one Sunday morning some years ago. The little boy was our five-year-old son, Jeff. "Which story?" I responded. "The one in your sermon about the little boy and the dog," Jeff answered. I knew then precisely what Jeff was asking about.

That Sunday morning, I had told a story about a little boy who came into a pet shop one day. He wanted to buy a puppy. When the little boy told the pet store owner about his interest in buying a dog, immediately the owner whistled loudly and four cute little puppies came running into the room, tails wagging, jumping excitedly, yipping happily. These little dogs were so engaging that even if you hadn't planned to buy a puppy, you would be reaching for your wallet. They were so irresistible! But then, at that moment, another little puppy came struggling into the room, limping noticeably and dragging one hind leg.

"What's the matter with that puppy, Mister?" the boy asked.

"Well, Son, that puppy is crippled. We took him to the vet and found that he was born with a bum leg. Unfortunately, the leg will never be right."

Quickly, the little boy pulled out his money and said boldly: "I'll take him! He's the one I want!"

"But, Son, you don't seem to understand," said the owner. "That puppy is going to be crippled all his life. They can't fix his leg. Why in the world would you want him when you can have one of these others . . . ?"

Before the owner could finish his question, the little boy reached down and pulled up his pants leg, revealing an iron brace holding his twisted leg. Then he said: "Mister, this puppy is going to need someone to help him. He's going to need someone who understands—and I am the one who understands. You see, he needs me and I need him!"

Well, that was the story I had told that Sunday morning that had prompted Jeff's question, "Daddy, is that story true, or were you just preaching?" With a nod to all the other preachers out there whose kids have asked them the same question, let's just say that Jeff had already learned that preachers do indeed sometimes "stretch the truth," or as someone once put it, they "remember big!"

I knew that a little boy like Jeff would naturally and easily relate to a story like that about a little boy and a puppy. But I also knew that he wanted and deserved an honest answer from his dad. So I said to him: "Well, Jeff, that is an excellent question, and it also shows that you listened well in church this morning, and that's great! I am always so proud of you! Let me try to answer your question like this. Preachers tell two different kinds of stories to get their points across. First, there are 'true stories,' and second, there are 'truth stories.' Both are good and helpful.

"True stories are stories about things that actually happened. They took place in history. They really occurred.

"On the other hand, a truth story is a story that teaches us a great truth. A truth story may not have actually happened in history, but it is a great story because it can teach us a helpful lesson about life. For example, Jesus' parables were probably truth stories. Was the story of the prodigal son a true story or a truth story? Well, we don't know for sure. Maybe Jesus knew a family who had had that experience, or maybe he created the story as a truth story to show us that God is a loving parent who runs down the road to welcome his son home with love and forgiveness. Either way, the story helps teach us an awesome lesson about God and life in God's family.

"So, I would answer your question about the little boy and the dog the same way. It may have actually happened, but more likely it is a 'once upon a time story,' a truth story that teaches us a good and helpful lesson. Does that answer your question?" And Jeff answered: "Cool!" And I was thrilled!

This book has both kinds of stories in it, true stories and truth stories, and my prayer is that the stories recorded here in these pages will indeed teach us valuable lessons about faith, hope, and love, but more (even more) hopefully, prayerfully, they will draw us closer to God and God's truth.

CHAPTER 1

GO OUT SINGING

ACTS 16:25-40

Have you ever noticed how God can use the most unlikely people to get his work done?

The musical *Go Out Singing* is a sequel to *Godspell*; it takes up where *Godspell* leaves off. Look at how powerfully and dramatically the play begins.

The *Go Out Singing* overture begins when the houselights have faded as usual. It has the sound of a Broadway overture, although slightly more dignified in tone.

After several of the show's tunes have been played, the overture dissolves into a long, high note, which continues to be held as the curtain rises on darkness and the beginning of Scene 1. As the curtain reaches its height, we hear a sound. It's the sound of a rooster crowing. Silence. It crows again.

The lights start coming up slowly, and we see the solitary figure of a man sitting on a rock, head in hands. Behind him, up left, are the gates leading into Jerusalem. Behind him, up right, far in the distance, are the silhouettes of three crosses with bodies on them.

The orchestra breaks from its single note with a soft, stinging chord. The man seated on the rock, Simon Peter, raises his head sadly and sings a song, "And Now This," in which he reflects upon how they had such great hope but now their hopes are dashed because the Lord has been crucified.

Later in the song, Peter sings of squandered chances and missed opportunities. Peter, who denied Christ three times, wishes for just one more chance. He is sure that this time, he would be "twice the man. . . . twice . . . no, thrice the man!"

That's what *Go Out Singing* is about—Simon Peter's second chance, the Resurrection, Pentecost, the healing of the sick, encounters with Paul and Nero, courage, obedience, persecution, imprisonment, martyrdom, the most unlikely people working against the most incredible odds and working against it all with a song of triumph. The title, *Go Out Singing*, connects to two fascinating episodes:

✦ First, Peter and John are in prison. The jailer is asleep, when suddenly, miraculously, the doors open. John whispers, "Let's slip out of here."

"No!" says Peter, "We are not going to slip out of anywhere. We are going to go out singing." Peter and John shake their chains in rhythm and they go out singing.

✦ Second, Peter, in the final scene, is being led out to be crucified upside down. His friends begin to cry. Peter stops and

says, "Don't weep for me . . . I'm gonna go out singing."
And he does.

When you see it, it will make you laugh, it will make you cry. It will touch you, challenge you, inspire you. But most of all, it will make you go out singing.

Speaking of how God can use the most unlikely people to do his work, consider the case of King James I of Great Britain. Quite possibly no other English king will be longer remembered.

This is most unusual because King James, especially in his later years, was morbidly afraid of death. He became so paranoid, so convinced that everyone was plotting against him, that he was cheerful only when he was drunk. So, he drank more and more to escape the fear. He seldom went to bed sober.

He probably would have been long forgotten as just another king of England—and not a very good one at that—except for one thing: He was responsible for the printing of the best-selling book of all time. It bears his name, the King James Version of the Bible.

In 1604, King James made a snap decision, prompted by an Oxford scholar named John Reynolds. It may well have been that Reynolds convinced King James to permit the printing of the Bible by appealing to his vanity. "Your name will be on it!"

Reflecting on this some years later, Bible scholar J. D. Douglas made a striking observation when he pointed out that the King James Version of the Bible is a dramatic reminder to us of God's amazing capacity for "writing straight with crooked lines."

I have often thought about that fascinating phrase, "writing straight with crooked lines," because it is just another way of saying that God often uses the most unlikely tools to achieve his purposes.

It is an interesting thing to ponder, isn't it? That is, how God uses unlikely people, unlikely events, unlikely tools to get his work done. Could it be possible that God might even use you and me?

‡‡‡‡‡‡‡‡‡‡‡‡‡‡‡‡‡‡‡‡‡‡‡‡‡‡‡‡‡‡‡‡‡

CHAPTER 2

IF YOU GET WHERE YOU ARE GOING, WHERE WILL YOU BE?

LUKE 15:11-24

Some years ago, well-known preacher Harry Emerson Fosdick told the story about a man who boarded a bus, fully intending to go to Detroit, but at the end of the long trip when he got off the bus he found himself not in Detroit, but in Kansas City.

He had caught the wrong bus!

Something like that happens repeatedly in life. People on the whole desire good things. Basically, we want happiness, maturity, and meaning. We want good marriages, productive careers, useful lives. We want poise, respect, an honorable old age, and strong faith.

Our intentions are good, but sometimes we catch the wrong bus and thus end up in the wrong place.

That man who started for Detroit, but instead landed in Kansas City, would not believe it at first. He got off the bus and asked for directions to Woodward Avenue. When he was told that there was no Woodward Avenue in this city, he was indignant.

"Now see here," he said, "I know Detroit, I have been to Detroit many times and I have been on Woodward Avenue in Detroit. Don't tell me there is no Woodward Avenue here!"

"But, sir, this is Kansas City," someone told him.

Finally, it dawned on him with a sickening thud that despite the clarity of his desire and his intention—he had, in fact, caught the wrong bus and he had, in fact, ended up in the wrong place.

This is a great parable for life, because it can happen to us. Think about it a moment.

The prodigal son didn't mean to end up in a swine pasture. That was not his intended destination. He wanted happiness, fulfillment, freedom. But he "caught the wrong bus" and wound up in the wrong place as a starving, defeated, deflated feeder of pigs.

Judas Iscariot didn't mean to end up a traitor. That was not his intended destination, but somehow it happened, and he has gone down in history as the man who sold out his master.

The rich young ruler didn't mean to end up sorrowful, but he "caught the wrong bus" and ended up in the wrong place.

Life is full of that experience. Over the years, I have had the privilege of officiating at the marriage ceremonies of hundreds of couples—charming, happy, attractive young couples (and some not so young) with great joy in their hearts and great hope in their eyes. You know they intend to have happy homes and good marriages.

But as the years pass, and I see so many marriages start for Utopia and end up in the divorce courts, I find myself at the marriage service offering up a silent prayer—"Oh, God, help them catch the right bus!"

I see parents who want so much for their children to have high morals and good values, but they don't spend enough time with their children or have enough discussions with them about things that really matter.

They want their children to have the best religious training, and yet they treat Sunday school lightly and seemingly relieve themselves from responsibility here.

You see, good intentions are not enough. This truth touches us personally too. Most of us desire good things—we want meaning and fulfillment. We want happiness and acceptance. We want respectable character and spiritual wisdom. We want a good prayer life and command of the Scriptures. We want respect from our friends and an old age unashamed.

The truth is that we have high ideals and good goals, but the critical question rises: Are we on the right bus? Are we on the road that leads where we want to go?

In our everyday conversations we have certain phrases that underscore this problem. We say things such as:

- ✦ "He is headed for a fall," or . . .
- ✦ "She is on a collision course," or . . .
- ✦ "He is off the track" or "out in left field."

What about you and me? Are we on the right road to get where we want to go? Are we doing the things to ensure that we will end up at our intended destination? Or are we on the wrong bus?

So, the question is a crucial one to think about—"If you get where you are going, where will you be?"

CHAPTER 3

++++++++++++++++++++++++++++++++++

IS IT SINFUL TO GET ANGRY?

MARK 11:15-19

It was late on a Monday afternoon. I was going through some things on my desk when I sensed someone's presence. Have you ever had that experience?

My back was to the door and I was absorbed in what I was doing, when suddenly I felt the presence of another person. I turned around and there at the door to my office stood a young woman.

She was crying quietly. She said, "Jim, I'm sorry about walking in like this, but I just had to talk to somebody." She went on to describe a family squabble that had just erupted over nothing really important.

It could have been avoided or handled differently, she admitted, but it hadn't been, and angry, hostile words and actions exploded through the house. "I got so mad," she said. "I was so angry that I lost control. I couldn't see straight. I lost my head—and now I'm so ashamed. I feel devastated."

She paused for a moment and then she said, "Is it sinful to get angry? It must be because my soul feels so deflated and empty now after my angry outburst."

Then she added, "Sometimes I feel like God has converted every part of me except my temper. I'm a Christian, I try to do what is right, but I must confess that I have a terrible temper. I can get so angry!"

Now, what do you think? What would you have told that young woman? Is it sinful to get angry? One thing is for sure: anger can be sinful. It can become a spiritual cancer. It can destroy us and devastate other people. It can disrupt families, ruin friendships, split churches, and start wars. Anger is a powerful force in human nature which we too often let run toward negative, destructive ends.

In the Sermon on the Mount, Jesus spoke of a forbidden anger. He condemned anger, but we also know that later, he, himself, got angry—angry enough to run the money changers out of the Temple. What are we to make of this? How do we reconcile these two? Was Jesus inconsistent?

To answer these hard questions, we need to recognize that there are several different kinds of anger. Below are three common varieties. Let's look at them and see if we can find ourselves somewhere between the lines.

FIRST, THERE IS "ADOLESCENT ANGER," which unfortunately is not confined to the adolescent period.

Sadly, grownups can have childish temperaments. Psychiatrists tell us that people who are short-tempered, hostile, and irritable are basically immature. They may be adults chronologically, but emotionally they may still be little children who want to scream and kick because they can't have their own way. Think about it.

+ There is the man who flies into a rage because his toast is burnt.
+ There is the woman who quits the club because her name was accidentally omitted from a list of committee members.
+ There is the teenager who runs to her room and slams the door and pouts because she isn't permitted to go to the slumber party.
+ There is the church member who quits the church because his announcement was left out of the bulletin.

Does this sound familiar? Be honest. Have you grown up? Or are you still the victim of adolescent anger? What makes you mad? Cold coffee? The ring in the bathtub? An improperly squeezed toothpaste tube? A traffic jam? Homework? A missed parking place?

Some people show by their tantrums that they have quite simply never grown up. Like little children, they have made themselves the center of the universe and when their world is crossed or shaken, they get cross and shaken! All through the Scriptures, we are warned about the sinful misuse of anger and we are urged to mature spiritually—to grow up!

SECOND, THERE IS BROODING, SEETHING ANGER. We can say without a doubt that this kind of anger is sinful, because it is anger seeking vengeance, anger that will not forgive. It is murderous, destructive, dangerous anger.

In the Greek language, there are two words for anger. There is *thumos*, which is anger that quickly blazes up and then quickly dies down. And, there is *orgé*, which is the anger that broods and seethes and looks for the chance to pay somebody back. There is nothing that will separate us from God and devastate our souls and bring hell into our lives more quickly than *orgé*. There's no question about it. It is as sinful as sin can get.

THIRD, THERE IS CONSTRUCTIVE ANGER— RIGHTEOUS INDIGNATION. As always, Jesus is our best example of righteous indignation. Two dramatic things can be said about his use of this emotion:

On the one hand, he was never upset by unkindness directed toward himself! He was never personally offended! He was criticized, questioned, rejected, accused falsely, lied about, pushed and shoved, taunted, beaten, spat upon, cursed at, and nailed to a cross. But all the way through, when he was reviled, he reviled not again. They did all that to him and when they finished, he said: "Father, forgive them!"

Let me add a quick note here. This does not mean that we should permit anyone to abuse us. If we are in an abusive situation, we should report that and get out of it as soon as possible. I am simply saying that Jesus' anger was never selfish and neither should ours be.

On the other hand, Jesus did get upset by injustices done to others! He did get upset when he saw other people being exploited or mistreated or cheated or hurt. When he saw a woman judged without mercy, he was upset. When he saw religious leaders place custom and tradition before human need, he was upset. When he saw people cheated in the Temple, he was so upset that he overturned the money changers' tables and drove them out.

Jesus was never upset by any unkindness directed toward himself, but he was upset by injustices directed toward others. Our problem is that, more often than not, we reverse this. We get personally offended and fail to see others being exploited or mistreated.

Be honest now. What makes you angry? In summary, someone put it like this: "You can tell the size of a person by the size of the thing that makes that person mad."

+++++++++++++++++++++++++++++++++++++++

CHAPTER 4

WHEN YOUR HEART IS BROKEN

MATTHEW 5:1-12

Sooner or later, heartache comes to all of us. Sooner or later, one way or another, all of us will get our hearts broken.

Sadness, sorrow, disappointment, mourning, grief—whatever you wish to call it—will rear its head and cover us over like a heavy blanket. The "broken heart" is a fact of living. We do need help in knowing how to deal with it, how to work through it, and how to grow on it.

What does faith say to us about the grief experience? How does faith help mend the broken heart?

There are, indeed, some special resources in the Christian faith that help bring healing to the hurt heart. Let me suggest a few ideas that I think can serve us well as we walk through the dark valley of sorrow.

FIRST, CLAIM THE FELLOWSHIP OF THE CHURCH. Let the arms of love of the church family surround you and support you. Let the prayers, the casseroles, the tender handshakes, the gentle hugs, the letters and cards and phone calls be means of strength for you.

Let the worship services be celebrations of faith and helpful reminders that no matter how alone you may feel in your heartache, you are not alone—God is with you! Nothing, not even death, can separate you from God and his love.

So, let the worship and fellowship of the church surround you and uphold you. No matter how hurt you may feel, no matter how painful the experience, come back to regular church events as soon as you can. Let the church be an integral part of the healing process.

SECOND, CLAIM THE NEW POWER OF HELPING OTHERS that only comes from having gone through the grief pilgrimage. Those who have gone through sorrow have a new empathy, a new sensitivity, a new compassion, a new power to do something for others.

In Matthew 5, Jesus said, "Blessed are those who mourn, for they will be comforted!"

Notice the word "comforted." It comes from two Latin words: *cum*, which means "with," and *fortis*, which means "strength." So, the word "comforted" literally means "with strength"! Thus, Jesus was saying: "Blessed are those who have gone through sorrow for they are 'with strength.'"

Albert Schweitzer put it like this: "Whoever among us has learned through personal experience what pain and anxiety really are . . . no longer belongs to himself alone; he has become the brother of all who suffer."

Therefore, claim the strength to help others that only comes on the other side of trouble, that only comes from walking through the valley of grief.

LAST, CLAIM THE PRESENCE OF GOD. The good news of our faith is that God is with us in every circumstance of life and indeed beyond this life. Early in his Gospel, when Matthew is trying to capture in a word the meaning of Jesus, he wisely comes up with the word "Emmanuel," which means "God with us."

The most important thing Jesus Christ shows us is Emmanuel! This means that God is with us and God is for us. God is a loving Father!

A few years ago, my brother Bob, a minister in Tennessee, sent me a copy of one of his sermons. In it was the touching story of a young man whose wife had died, leaving him with a small son.

Back home from the cemetery, they went to bed as soon as dark came because there was nothing else he could think of that he could bear to do. As he lay there in the darkness—broken-hearted, grief-stricken, numb with sorrow—the little boy broke the stillness from his little bed with a disturbing question: "Daddy, where is Mommy?"

The father tried to get the boy to go to sleep, but the questions kept coming from the little boy's confused mind. After a while, the father got up and brought the little boy to bed with him. But the child was still disturbed and restless and occasionally would ask a probing, heartbreaking question.

Finally, the little boy reached out his hand through the darkness and placed it on his father's face asking: "Daddy, is your face toward me?"

Assured verbally and by his own touch that his father's face was indeed toward him, the little boy said, "If your face is toward me, I think I can go to sleep." And in a little while he was quiet.

The father lay there in the darkness and in childlike faith lifted up his own needy heart to his Father in heaven and prayed something like this: "Oh God, the way is dark and I confess that I do not see my way through, but if your face is toward me, somehow I think I can make it."

CHAPTER 5

SHOULD I FORGIVE?

LUKE 23:32-38

A certain writer once shared a truth he had learned on a trip to Yellowstone National Park. A ranger took him to a clearing where grizzly bears were fed. As they watched the grizzlies eating, the ranger talked about how powerful the grizzly bear is.

"The grizzly can whip any animal in the West," he said, "with the possible exception of the buffalo and the Kodiak bear."

Not long after the ranger had made that statement, the writer noticed something that fascinated him. All the other animals gave way to the grizzly. All the other animals moved aside, got out of the way, but one—a small furry animal was confident and unafraid and stood right there and ate alongside the huge bear. The grizzly never challenged him.

The fearless animal was not a buffalo or a Kodiak bear. It was a little black and white skunk!

Of course, the grizzly could have easily won in a fight with the skunk. Of course, the grizzly could have easily crushed the life out of the skunk with one paw. But the grizzly didn't touch the skunk.

Why? Because he knew he would have to pay too high a price.

That is a smart grizzly! In fact, he is smarter than many of us humans who spend weary days and sleepless nights:

+ Brooding over our resentments
+ Calculating ways of getting even
+ Demanding our pound of flesh
+ Seething over our grievances
+ Wallowing in our self-pity
+ Unbending in not giving mercy
+ Being unable to forgive and forget.

Remember the story about the man who began to think about getting a divorce? He went to a lawyer to talk about his marital problem and after telling his side of the story asked, "What is the best thing I can do?"

The attorney replied: "The best thing you can do is go home. Go back to your wife, apologize to her; pledge to her your undying love, and make this marriage work. That's the best thing you can do!"

The man was silent, then said: "What is the next best thing I can do?"

We had just as well admit it. Broken relationships, hostility, and violence blight our world and reduce the meaning of life for everyone involved.

In a way, we are a bundle of contradictions. On the one hand, we need each other and I think most people really want to get along. But communication falters, suspicion creeps in, and we end up misunderstanding, hurting, and frustrating one another.

Resentment, anger, jealousy, selfishness poison us, and we say things and do things that separate people and break hearts. Or else we treat each other with cold indifference and remain remote and inaccessible.

This is why a prominent emphasis on Jesus' teaching centers on *forgiveness*. He knew that no love, no marriage, no friendship, no family, no church, and no society can live without it.

+ A cruel word is finally only an echo.
+ Revenge is never sweet; it ultimately becomes a sour stomach and bitter memory.
+ Violence only breeds more violence.
+ Hate poisons the soul.

Jesus knew this and thus he called for us to be bridgebuilders, to be peacemakers, to seek forgiveness and to offer it.

This was a key theme of many of his parables!

This is a dominant theme in the Sermon on the Mount.

This is the major theme of his life.

If you ever wonder "Should I forgive this person who has hurt me?"—if that question ever comes up—just remember the picture of Jesus on the cross saying, "Father . . . Forgive them!"

Theologian Horace Bushnell put it like this: "Forgiveness is man's deepest need and highest achievement."

◆◆◆◆◆◆◆◆◆◆◆◆◆◆◆◆◆◆◆◆◆◆◆◆◆◆◆◆◆◆◆◆◆◆

CHAPTER 6

WHEN IT'S HARD TO BELIEVE

MARK 9:14-29

Is it wrong to wonder? Is it sinful to doubt? Is it bad to raise questions about our faith?

In *A Spiritual Autobiography*, Dr. William Barclay said that "some people are what you might call 'natural believers,'" meaning that belief is easier for some people than for others.

On the other hand, there are people who find it hard to believe, and I guess all of us have moments when we want to cry out with the man in the Gospels, "Lord, I believe, help thou my unbelief!"

What about you? Is it easy or hard for you to believe? Do you ever feel that your faith is not as strong as you would like it to be? The great preacher Dr. Leonard Griffith once said that there are two kinds of skeptics where religion is concerned:

First, there are those who don't believe and don't care, and there is not much you can do for them until such an attitude is changed. On one of our college campuses some years ago, the college newspaper offered a prize for the best definition of life. Some of the answers were negative and discouraging: "Life is a bad joke which isn't even funny." "Life is a disease for which the only cure is death." "Life is a jail sentence which we get for the crime of being born." Now, there is not much you can do with that kind of cynical, bitter skepticism.

On the other hand, there is a second group of what Griffith called "honest doubters"—people who want to believe, but find it hard to do so. "These people," said Dr. Griffith, "get close to me and their hurt becomes my hurt." I join in that concern. What do you say to those people who want to believe, yet somehow find it hard to do so?

Remember that man in Mark's Gospel? Here is a father worried sick over his son who has for several years had terrible seizures rendering him speechless, knocking him to the ground and making him foam at the mouth, grind his teeth, and go rigid all over.

Imagine the concern of this father. He has tried everything. He wants so much for his son to be made well. He brings him to Jesus and says, "Please help us, if you can." Jesus answers, "If you can! All things are possible to him who believes!"

Notice the desperation of that father as he cries out: "I believe; help my unbelief!" In other words, "I'm believing as much as I can. . . . Please make up for my inadequate faith." Then, as you remember from the story, Jesus heals the boy.

Now, my heart goes out to that father and to people like him who want so to believe, but find it hard. What do we say to them? What do we do ourselves when we come to the place in life where it is hard to believe? Let me suggest a few things to remember when it is hard to believe.

FIRST, REMEMBER THAT OUR BELIEFS WILL ALWAYS BE CHALLENGED and that we can't permit ourselves to be so insecure that we are shaken by every ripple or confusion or question. The truth is that sometimes these challenges are stepping stones to growth. They force us to think through our beliefs more seriously.

Sometimes these challenges are painful, but growing pains do seem to be an inevitable part of maturing. God gave us minds and surely we were meant to use them. I have never known a mature Christian who at some point did not raise questions about his faith and then set out to find the answers.

I have a minister friend who purposefully listens to a radio preacher whom he disagrees with greatly. They are poles apart theologically. Their approach to faith is totally different. My friend listens to the preacher he disagrees with as a "discipline in thinking," asking himself as he listens: "Why do I see that differently? What do I really believe about this? Why is my approach different?" He says this exercise has helped him greatly in coming to fresh new insights in the Christian faith.

In a word, our faith should not stifle our questions and our questions should not stifle our faith. Rather, questions may be the means by which our faith grows and deepens.

SECOND, REMEMBER THE PEOPLE YOU KNOW OF WHO BELIEVE. Remember the great cloud of witnesses, the company of the committed.

The most fulfilled, productive, creative, joyous people I know of personally and historically have been believers, and that is reassuring. Think of it: Abraham, Moses, David, Jeremiah, Isaiah, Peter, Paul, Luther, Calvin, Wesley, Francis of Assisi, Mother Teresa, Dietrich Bonhoeffer, Paul Tillich, Wernher von Braun, David Livingstone, Phillips Brooks, Albert Schweitzer, the people in your church congregation—and Jesus of Nazareth.

I'd like to take my stand with all of them and with Jesus.

THIRD, WHEN IT'S HARD TO BELIEVE, REMEMBER THE CHURCH: what it is, what it stands for, what it represents—the best there is in the world. I know the church has its weaknesses, but I also wish that I had more than one life to give to the church.

FOURTH, REMEMBER THAT DOUBTS ABOUT NONESSENTIAL MATTERS CAN BLIND US TO THE REAL ESSENTIAL. That is, some people worry over things that don't matter that much and thereby miss the things that do matter much.

Does it really make any difference what the dimensions of heaven are, how the streets are paved, what the temperature of hell is, or what color the hymnbooks should be? We can toy with nonessentials and miss the main things.

FIFTH, WHEN IT'S HARD TO BELIEVE, REMEMBER THAT FAITH IS CONFIRMED BY THE LIVING OF IT. Faith is strengthened by practice. Jesus didn't say memorize these doctrines. He said "Follow me!"

+++

CHAPTER 7

TALKING A GOOD GAME IS NOT ENOUGH

MICAH 6:6-8

When it comes to religion we talk a pretty good game most of the time. Our problem in faith matters is not so much with words as with actions—or maybe better put, the lack of action.

We tend to talk so much and do so little. We tend to verbalize well and actualize so poorly. We often speak high-sounding words into the air and then put off acting until tomorrow.

But we must see—we must—that "talking a good game is simply not enough." Only when our words are translated into actions are they authenticated. Nowhere is this truer than with matters of faith. It is not enough to preach it from our pulpits or sing it in our hymns. Faith is a lifestyle—a way of living. Faith is not merely a set of intellectual ideas or theological beliefs or philosophical arguments; it is a way of acting and responding to life, to people, to God.

Faith is not just a way of believing; it is also a way of behaving. Faith is not just something we proclaim and celebrate in the sanctuary, it is something we live out and demonstrate and share with others at home, in the office, on the street, on the tennis court, on a date.

Recently, I ran across a story about something that happened some years ago. A plow was sent to Africa and fell into the possession of a tribe in the interior of the continent. The people had never seen a plow before. They didn't know what the strange-looking instrument was and so not knowing what else to do with it, they set it up on a pedestal and worshiped it!

That plow, of course, was designed to be used, not revered. It was designed to strike deep into the African soil and prepare it for the production of fruit and grain and vegetables. It was designed to nourish people, to make them healthier, to make their quality of life better; but the members of that tribe didn't know that, so they made the plow an ornament rather than a tool.

This is what we are tempted to do with our faith—to make it an ornament rather than a tool, to think of it as an object of veneration rather than a means to personal and social transformation, to see it as a lovely set of ideals to be laid neatly upon a pedestal rather than as a force designed to revolutionize one's manner of life and the whole fabric of society.

That was what so upset the prophets in the eighth century before Christ. Amos, Micah, Hosea, and Isaiah cried out dramatically because they felt, and rightly so, that unless your faith touches your moral behavior, it is a farce; unless your religion changes your life, it is just so much hypocritical play acting.

Liturgies, ceremonies, and holy feasts were good, the prophets believed, if they produced righteous lives. Otherwise, they were a stench in the nostrils of God.

The point is that "talking a good game is not enough." Unless our creeds become deeds, they become dull, insipid, dead, worthless. If we don't practice what we preach, then it is but "sound and fury, signifying nothing." Only when our creeds become deeds do they become compelling, contagious, and convincing. The supreme argument for holy faith is a holy life. Edgar Guest put it poetically:

> I'd rather see a sermon than hear one any day,
> I'd rather one should walk with me than merely show the way.

CHAPTER 8

YOU HAVE TO FINISH WHAT YOU START

JOHN 19:28-30

Some years ago when I was in high school, I enjoyed running track. I was a sprinter for the team at Tech High in Memphis, Tennessee, and I ran the 100-yard dash and the 220 and also did some field events such as the long jump.

But more than anything I got a kick out of being on the sprint relay teams. There was something very special to me about being a part of a team, that camaraderie, that spirit, that closeness that comes from working together like a well-tuned, synchronized machine; that unique fellowship that comes from winning and losing together, from rejoicing and hurting together, from laughing and crying together.

We had a good 880-yard relay team. Each runner would run 220 yards, then hand the baton at full speed to the next man, who would then run his leg of the race and hand the baton to the next man until all four runners had completed the 880-yard distance. We had a fine team and we came through all of our meets undefeated to the day of the regional track meet. All we had to do was finish in the top three to win a trip to the state meet in Knoxville.

Earlier in the season we had defeated every team in the race. We were confident—maybe even a bit cocky. We had already made plans for our trip to Knoxville. Then came time for the race, the 880-yard relay.

We were primed and ready. Our first runner jumped out front and got us a good lead. Our second runner increased it. I was next and when I passed the baton to our anchor man, we had a 40-yard lead.

As I stood and watched our last runner coming out of the final turn—way in front—I began to think about the medals we were going to win, the trophy that would be placed in the trophy case at school with our names on it, our pictures in the paper, the trip to Knoxville, and the opportunity to run in the state track meet.

Suddenly, I was brought back to reality. Our anchor man, just 35 yards short of the finish, pulled a muscle and fell down. As he lay there, holding his leg, writhing in pain, one by one, the other teams passed him by and instead of first place, we came in last.

That quickly, it was all over. I can remember, as if it were yesterday, the sick feeling in the pit of my stomach—concern and empathy for my injured teammate and hurt over our lost opportunity.

But I learned a valuable lesson that day about life. I learned dramatically how important it is to finish—to finish what you start. It's not enough to make a good start. It's not enough to just run well. It's not enough to "wow the crowd." You have to finish. You have to see it through or it is all to no avail.

Harry Emerson Fosdick said it well:

> A very serious test of human fiber is involved in the fact that there are so many good beginnings and poor endings. . . . Good starters and good stayers are not necessarily the same people. Ardor, excitement, feeling, the flare of good intentions—such forces set men going, but they do not enable men to carry on when the going is hard. That requires another kind of moral energy which evidently is not so common as the first.
>
> Plenty of people get away easily. They are off with fleet eagerness that wakens high expectations, but they peter out; they soon stick in the sand or stall on a high hill.
>
> In one of our federal prisons today is a man who for fifty years with unblemished reputation lived a life of . . . honor in his own community. Then, as a government servant, he went to France during the war and mishandled funds. Only that will be remembered about him. The half-century of fine living is blotted out. He was not able to finish.

The great people of history were persons with power to see it through. Einstein, Churchill, Lincoln, Edison, Helen Keller—all had reasons to quit, but they didn't.

Through determination and commitment they persisted, endured, persevered. Against this backdrop, the words of Jesus ring out even more powerfully as we see him hanging there on a cross and saying with his last breath, "It is finished. I have seen it through."

++++++++++++++++++++++++++++++++++++

CHAPTER 9

A BAD CASE OF THE SIMPLES

MARK 10:17-22

Some years ago, the late Senator Thomas Hart Benton was asked what was most difficult about being a U.S. senator. His answer was interesting.

He said the hardest thing for him to deal with was the frustrating fact that his constituents back in Missouri had a "bad case of the simples"—they expected him to work "instant miracles" in Washington.

They so easily reduced all complexities to very neat little black and white simplicities. He said they didn't seem to realize that the most meaningful and significant accomplishments take time, effort, commitment, sacrifice, discipline, and perseverance.

Senator Benton was on target. The plain fact is that nothing—nothing!—in this world is simple, if by simple we mean easy to grasp. A blade of grass is not a simple thing nor is a teardrop or a snowflake or an atom or an electron or a love feeling. Take three steps into anything and you're in an ocean over your head in mystery.

I read recently about a man who wanted a revelation from God. "I want a revelation," the man kept saying. "I want God to speak to me simple and straight."

Finally, his pastor said to him, "The next time it rains, go outside, look up in the heavens, and ask God for a revelation." A few days later after a good soaking rain, the man came back to his pastor. He was sopping wet. "I followed your advice," he said. "Stood in the rain for over an hour, looking up into the skies and asking for a revelation from God, but no revelation from God. The rain pelted my face, the water ran down my neck, and I felt ignorant and stupid."

To which the pastor replied, "What greater revelation do you want?"

Most of us don't have to stand in the rain to realize how uninformed we are in this complex universe. Even Thomas Edison, as knowledgeable as he was, said, "We don't know the millionth part of one percent about anything."

So, there's no use asking for a simple religion. Dr. Hal Luccock said, "I don't know who first coined the phrase, 'The Simple Gospel.' I hope that God, being slow to anger and plenteous in mercy has forgiven them, but the evil they did lives after them. For hiding under that innocent phrase, 'The Simple Gospel,' is usually a distorted, deluded message picking out a few factors and leaving out all the rest."

We must beware of oversimplification. The things in life that really matter do not come quickly, easily, or simply. They take time, effort, sacrifice, and commitment.

To be sure, some things you can get immediately, by pushing buttons or paying money down or pulling out a plastic card. But the great things, the real values, do not come that way. They have to be grown and cultivated. You can get a sports car or a color TV with a quick down payment, but character, morality, values, faith, maturity, spiritual strength—these you have to wait for, want, commit to, and grow slowly but surely.

For example, developing a meaningful prayer life is no simple matter. It doesn't happen overnight. It doesn't come instantly or magically. It just takes a lot of time and a lot of practice.

The missionary Florence Allshorn said, "There is really only one test of our prayer life. Namely, do we want God? Do we want him so much that we'll go on and on if it takes five, six, ten years to find him?"

If you want to become a doctor, lawyer, minister, teacher, musician, or an athlete, it takes effort and determination. It doesn't come easily or simply. Maybe the same is true with prayer. Maybe it just takes a lot of practice.

Or, think of the Scriptures. Developing a meaningful understanding of the Scriptures is no simple matter. The truth is that while the Bible is in nearly all of our homes, not all of us are at home in it.

Edward Blair in *The Bible and You* pointed out, "The person who is looking for a way to master the Bible in three easy lessons will be disappointed. In the first place, one can never master the Bible; one can only be mastered by it. In the second place, the Bible is so incalculably rich that the human mind cannot possibly embrace it all in a few attempts. Familiarity with the Bible comes only by long exposure to its contents."

Being a real disciple is no simple matter. It is a growing, developing thing. It is a wonderful thing to become a "newborn," but to remain a spiritual baby is tragic. Babies are sweet and adorable, but if they remain infants and never grow up, we consider that a calamity, and it is.

Becoming a real disciple is an ongoing process, a pilgrimage, a life commitment. It's not simple or easy; we have to practice, practice, practice.

CHAPTER 10

ROADBLOCKS

ROMANS 15:22-23

It had happened again. I was running late, rushing through traffic on my way to an appointment to speak at a local high school. Zipping along down a crowded major urban thoroughfare, thinking over what I was going to say to a group of teachers on the subject of dealing with stress creatively, I realized that I had again put myself under stress by starting out too late.

"Why didn't I leave sooner?" I muttered, fussing at myself.

Nervously, I glanced at my watch as I approached a congested intersection. I was due to speak in five minutes. "If all goes well, if I hit the traffic lights just right, I might make it," I thought to myself.

A sigh of relief eased past my lips a few moments later as I came in sight of the school. I could see my destination!

Now, all I had to do was top a hill, make one more turn, then get into the parking lot, jog across the campus, and I would be there in the auditorium just on time—maybe even a whole minute early.

But then as I came over that last hill, I couldn't believe my eyes. The road was closed . . . dug up . . . barricaded off. I could see where I wanted to go, but couldn't get there.

What a frustration! I could see my destination, but the road (the only one I knew) was closed off. After a long series of twists, turns, and abortive attempts (along with having to stop and ask directions three times), I finally made it—twenty minutes late. Was I ever personally prepared to speak authoritatively on the subject of stress!

I thought of that stressful situation and that closed-road experience again recently as I was studying Paul's Letter to the Romans. There is a poignant verse there that relates to frustrating closed roads. Paul says to the Romans, "I hope to see you in passing when I go to Spain."

"When I go to Spain," Paul said. More than anything, he wanted to go to Spain to take the church there. He had his heart set on that! He wanted to take the gospel to the outermost rim of the known world, but he never got there. The road closed for him. Instead, he got a prison cell in Rome.

His experience has something to say to us because all of us know the frustration of closed roads. We all have to deal with disappointments. We all have to handle disrupted plans, deferred hopes, unrealized dreams, and aggravating detours.

As J. Wallace Hamilton put it, "Every man's life is a diary in which he means to write one story and is forced to write yet another."

Well, what do we do when the road closes before us? Over the years, people have made several different responses to the frustration of closed roads.

Some get angry, but that doesn't really help.

Some wallow in self-pity, but that doesn't really help.

Some quit the journey, but that doesn't really help.

Some try to find someone to blame, but that doesn't really help.

Well, how do we respond to closed roads? Paul helped us here. We can do what he did. Namely, we can *find another way*. This is the creative response of faith, isn't it?

Paul wanted to go to Spain, but the road closed and instead he went to a prison cell in Rome. What a frustration! What a disappointment! But look how Paul responded. He found another way.

He sat down in that prison cell, took pen in hand, and began to scribble out some words on a bit of parchment. And those words became much of what we now call the New Testament. After twenty years of being constantly on the move, Paul at last had time . . . time in a prison cell, time to think, time to penetrate deeply into the mysteries of faith . . . and time to write it down!

It if had not been for Paul's roadblock, we would be the poorer. His words made it not only to Spain, but further still than Paul ever could have imagined!

Out of that disappointment came some of Paul's greatest contributions to the world, simply because when one road closed Paul would not content himself with anger, self-pity, quitting, or blame-placing. No, he found another way, and God, in the miracle of his grace, made it a better way.

History is full of that experience.

Edison wanted to sell newspapers on a train, but that road closed and he found telegraphy and scientific research.

Lincoln felt he was a total failure at age forty-six, but he looked for another way and that way led to the White House.

Whistler wanted to be a solider, but that road closed when he flunked chemistry at West Point. He then turned to art.

Edgar Bergen sent off for a book on photography, but got instead a book on ventriloquism.

Jesus of Nazareth, at the height of his ministry, was nailed to a cross in his early thirties, but God turned that horrid event into his greatest victory.

So, if you miss your Spain, if your road is blocked, don't get discouraged. Just remember that God may have a better road for you to travel.

CHAPTER 11

SOME THINGS ARE WORTH SAYING OVER AND OVER

MATTHEW 7:24-29

There are some things worth repeating. There are some things worth saying over and over and worth hearing again and again.

Benjamin Franklin believed that when he published the first edition of *Poor Richard's Almanack* in 1733 and continued to publish it for twenty-six years.

Poor Richard had all the usual features of almanacs, including astrological predictions, jokes, verses, and fiction. But the almanac was most famous for its wise sayings. Franklin himself said that he assembled the wisdom of many ages and nations into these proverbs, which he obviously felt were worth saying over and over.

Some were wise, some were witty, and some were both—"God helps them that help themselves." "A penny saved is a penny earned." "Little strokes fell great oaks." "He's a fool that makes his doctor his heir." "He that falls in love with himself will have no rivals."

Wise sayings such as these have been with us since time began. Proverbs, which tell a helpful truth or some bit of useful wisdom in short picturesque sentences, seem to be a part of every language and every people's heritage.

The Old Testament contains an entire book of Proverbs and additional wisdom literature with fascinating sayings that have been handed down from generation to generation. Sayings such as—"A soft answer turns away wrath"; "The fear of the Lord is the beginning of wisdom"; and "A good name is to be chosen rather than great riches."

Also, thousands of years ago, Roman philosopher Cicero gave us some words that have been repeated millions of times since he first spoke them: "One does not have to believe everything he hears" and "Virtue is its own reward."

When you stop and think about it, you see that the Ten Commandments are, in a sense, wise sayings that Moses and the early Israelites felt were worth repeating, worth saying over and over, and worth hearing again and again.

Nowadays we still do it. We pass on ideas that we want repeated in contemporary ways—with graffiti, billboards, commercials, banners, e-mail messages, tweets, and bumper stickers. Ideas such as "Today is the first day of the rest of your life," "Make my words sweet and tender today for I may have to eat them tomorrow," and "If life hands you a lemon, make a refreshing lemonade."

With the importance of proverbs and wise sayings in mind, it's interesting to look back at the teachings of Jesus to discover what key ideas he felt were worth repeating. I did this recently and noticed that three major thoughts emerged over and over, namely:

1. PEOPLE ARE MORE IMPORTANT THAN THINGS. Jesus underscored that point repeatedly. People matter, he said to us over and over again. People are more important than laws or systems, more important than things. According to Jesus, things are to be used and people are to be loved. That has to be repeated, because we are so prone not only to forget it but to reverse it—using people and loving things. But Jesus brings us up short by saying it again and again. People are more important than things and the best way to show our love for God is to love his children.

2. DISCIPLESHIP IS COSTLY. Over and over he said it. You can't be a person of faith and live by the law of selfishness. That's a contradiction. Discipleship means dying to selfishness and coming alive to self-givingness. Deny yourself, take up your cross, count the cost, follow me. The price is high, but it's worth it. As has been said, "The only thing more costly than caring is not caring."

3. GOD IS A LOVING FATHER (not an angry, hostile, vindictive deity who must be appeased). More than anything else, this is what Jesus came to teach us. He came not to change God's mind but to reveal it. Over and over, he painted God's portrait with strokes of love as the gracious, merciful, forgiving, compassionate father.

That is the good news and it's worth saying and hearing over and over.

CHAPTER 12

THE CHOICE IS YOURS: YOU CAN BUILD UP OR TEAR DOWN

MATTHEW 5:9

Some years ago, I realized something that I believe is very important.

In living, we have a choice. We can build up, or we can tear down. The happy people are those who understand that we have the choice and then choose to build up.

This, of course, is what the seventh Beatitude is about. When Jesus said "Blessed are the peacemakers, for they will be called children of God," what he meant was, "How happy and fulfilled are the peacemakers for they will be doing a God-like work."

Commenting on this Beatitude, William Barclay points out:

> There are people who are always storm-centers of trouble and bitterness and strife. Wherever they are, they are either in quarrels themselves or the cause of quarrels between others. They are troublemakers. There are people like that in almost every society . . . and such people are doing the devil's own work.

On the other hand . . . thank God . . . there are people in whose presence bitterness cannot live, people who bridge the gulfs and heal the breaches and sweeten the bitternesses. Such people are doing a God-like work for it is the great purpose of God, to bring peace. . . . The one who divides people is doing the work of evil; the one who unites people is doing God's work.

So, you see, the choice is yours. You can be a troublemaker or a peacemaker. You can build up or you can tear down!

Let me illustrate the point with four related ideas.

FIRST, YOU CAN ENCOURGE OR YOU CAN DISCOURAGE. More than anything now, the world needs a word of hope, a word of encouragement. When will we ever learn? People don't want to be put down; they are crying out to be lifted up.

In *You Are Not the Target*, author Laura Huxley puts it well when she says: "At one time or another the more fortunate among us make three startling discoveries." First, "each one of us has, in varying degree, the power to make others feel better or worse." Second, "making others feel better is much more fun than making them feel worse." Third, "making *others* feel better generally makes *us* feel better."

SECOND, YOU CAN SOOTHE OR YOU CAN SEETHE. In my opinion, there is nothing more destructive to our souls than seething resentment. It's a spiritual cancer. It can ruin your life. It can make you sick.

Paul Tournier, in *A Doctor's Casebook*, tells of treating a woman for anemia without success. Suddenly she was completely well. Miraculously she was healed. Intrigued by this, Dr. Tournier asked, "Has anything out of the ordinary happened in your life since I saw you last?" "Yes," she said, "I forgave someone against whom I had borne a nasty grudge for a long time; we reconciled! We are friends again and all at once I felt I could say 'Yes' to life!"

Isn't that something? Her seething had made her ill. When she stopped seething and gave her energy to soothing the situation, the impact was so great that it actually changed the physical state of her blood and made her well!

THIRD, YOU CAN LAUGH OR YOU CAN LAMENT. Isn't it tragic that so many people go through life feeling sorry for themselves? This is sad because God meant life to be joyous. A good sense of humor has never hurt a single person, and it has made life blossom like a flower in the desert for many. Abraham Lincoln, speaking of the pressures of being president, said, "With the fearful strain that is on me night and day, if I did not laugh from time to time, I would surely die."

FOURTH, YOU CAN PARDON OR YOU CAN PUNISH. What gets into us? Why do we think we need to punish people?

Some time ago, a man came to see me. The weekend before, he and his wife had gone to Dallas to celebrate their anniversary. As they were heading out of town, he remembered something he needed to take care of at his office. He turned back, went to his office, made the necessary arrangements, and then they were on their way, having lost only fifteen minutes with their stop.

But for some reason the stop made his wife furious. They drove to Dallas in silence. They endured a miserable weekend. She refused to speak to him. When he tried to talk, she turned away. When he tried to touch her, she pushed him away.

A week had passed when he came to see me. "She still won't speak to me," he said. "She won't listen to reason, she is still punishing me!"

Isn't that tragic? Why do we punish those we love in such cruel ways? It's so much better to pardon and forgive.

It's so much better to be a peacemaker.

You can tear down or you can build up. The choice is yours.

◆◆

CHAPTER 13

THE MEASURING STICK IS LOVE

JOHN 13:34-35

While on a recent speaking engagement in a college town, I slipped into a restaurant for a late-night sandwich. As I sat there by myself far from my home and my family, I felt a twinge of loneliness.

But then the people in the booth across from me began to talk about religion. I perked up. I didn't mean to eavesdrop, but there was no way to avoid their conversation.

They were three college coeds in their early twenties and talking about ethics, morality, goodness. Two of them—a few years before—had had dramatic, emotional religious experiences. Later, they had toured as members of a gospel team, appearing at youth rallies and retreats to give their testimonies.

Now, with a pitcher of beer in the middle of their table and wearing T-shirts with irreverent sayings (one read, "Instant Sex—Got a Minute?"), they were talking about religion. They were laughing about their old days of religious fervor and glorying in their new freedom. They were so glad that they had "outgrown" their earlier set of beliefs and naïve moral standards.

True, things weren't as simple as they once had thought. There is so much confusion, frustration, and discouragement in these hectic, pressure-packed days. One girl said, "We were wrong. Things aren't that easy. Things aren't that black and white any more; they are a muddled gray."

As I sat in that restaurant that night and accidentally overheard those girls in conversation, it dawned on me that in that brief life vignette, the moral dilemma of our time was highlighted and capsuled in interesting ways.

For one thing, a particular kind of narrow religion had failed these girls. It had not been realistic enough, tuned in enough, relevant enough to prepare them for a turbulent adult world where moral standards are confused and traditional beliefs are challenged. Their first brush with religion had not prepared them to know what goodness really is and what faith is about.

For another thing, they made one of the most common and most tragic mistakes you can make in the religious arena—they assumed that because one brand of religion didn't work that no religion works.

In outgrowing one kind of religion, the girls made the false assumption that they had bypassed the need for any kind of religion. The pendulum had swung too far from one extreme to another—from narrow, negative religion to no religion at all; from rigid legalism to loose libertinism; and from the heavy "thou shalt nots" to the giddy "anything you can get by with is permissible."

This all raises a significant question: How do you test the validity of a religious experience? How do you know if what you are feeling is a shallow emotionalism or a genuine faith experience?

In my opinion, the measuring stick is love.

If the experience makes me a more loving, caring person, then it is valid; if not, then it is suspect. That is, some people "get religion" but it is bad religion—narrow religion that makes them closed-minded, harsh, holier-than-thou, or even cruel. This kind of religious experience would not score well on the love measuring stick.

As I see it, religious experiences are authenticated by love. Jesus put it this way: "I give you a new commandment, that you love one another. Just as I have loved you, you also should love one another. By this everyone will know that you are my disciples, if you have love for one another." And Paul said, "If I speak in the tongues of mortals and of angels, but do not have love, I am a noisy gong or a clanging cymbal. And if I have prophetic powers, and understand all mysteries and all knowledge, and if I have all faith, so as to remove mountains, but do not have love, I am nothing."

CHAPTER 14

ARE YOU BUILDING BRIDGES OR WALLS?

EPHESIANS 2:11-22

Some years ago, I saw some young people present a special play one Sunday evening. The play was called *Construction*.

The production opens with a group of people gathered in an other-worldly kind of place.

They don't know where they are, or how they got there, or what they are supposed to do.

They discuss this: Where are we? Why are we in this place? What is our purpose here? What are we supposed to do? Who put us here?

At this point, they notice that there are some building materials there, so they decide that they obviously are supposed to build something.

But what?

Someone in the group wants to build a swimming pool. Another wants to build a hospital or an infirmary.

But then someone in the group says: "We are not alone here. Other people are around. I have been hearing the noises of other people. We don't know who they are or what these others are like . . . or what they are up to . . . and we can't afford to take a chance. It's too risky . . . we need to get a wall up before it's too late."

As they discuss this further, they become more and more frightened and decide that he is right: they should build a wall to protect themselves from those people out there. So, they organize and begin to build a formidable wall.

After they have worked for some time on their wall, they look up one day to see someone coming their way. When the stranger arrives, he tells them that he is a builder and that the one who put them there sent him to help them . . . and that he has the blueprints to show them what they are supposed to build!

Then, he tells them that they are not supposed to build a wall. Rather, they are supposed to build a bridge—a bridge to bring people together—not a wall to shut them out.

Upon hearing this, the group is enraged. They become angry with the builder—and suspicious.

Who is this man? Who does he think he is disrupting our plans like that? After all, our wall is almost finished.

"Wait a minute," they say. "Maybe he is a spy. Maybe he is trying to trap us." In a frenzied panic, they decide that the builder is a troublemaker and that they must get rid of this troublemaker with the blueprints.

They all charge and attack him.

At this point in the play, the lights go out, the organ swells and rumbles loudly, the group shouts hostilities, followed by complete silence and darkness.

Then a single spotlight comes on to reveal that the young builder who wanted them to build a bridge—rather than a wall—has been crucified.

The play ends as the group shrinks back in horror at what they have done. Then, quietly and shamefully, one of the characters says:

"We have to learn; we just have to learn. We can't go on crucifying the TRUTH forever!"

Now, this, to me, is a very powerful play. It's an unusual but relevant play for us right now because all about us people are still building walls—walls constructed of fear and pride and anxiety, walls made of prejudice and closed minds, walls that separate people and spread suspicion, walls that fence us in and shut others out.

But the good news of the play is that Jesus Christ is the young builder with the blueprints—and his truth can't be killed. It won't die; it resurrects. The truth is that he wants us to tear down our walls. The truth is that he wants us to be bridge builders.

CHAPTER 15

TRULY, THIS MAN WAS GOD'S SON!

MATTHEW 27:45-54

The Roman centurion saw it; he saw the truth as he stood at the foot of the cross. Jesus had just breathed his last, and as the Roman centurion looked up at the Nazarene, his mind darted back over the dramatic crescendo of events which had happened rapid-fire over the last few hours and days.

- ✦ He had seen Jesus riding into Jerusalem on a donkey with palm branches strewn before him, recognized as a king and yet not interested in earthly kingdoms.
- ✦ He had heard him teaching with keen insight and authority in public places.
- ✦ He had seen him arrested, falsely accused and convicted, mocked, jeered, slapped, spat upon.
- ✦ He had seen him brutally crucified—and noticed that he never struggled: He never said a "mumblin' word."

✦ He had heard him pray a prayer for forgiveness in behalf of his executioners.

✦ He had seen him console the thief on the adjacent cross.

✦ He had seen him make provisions for the care of his mother, even as he was in anguish on a cross.

✦ And now, the Roman centurion had seen Jesus of Nazareth die, and as he looked up at Jesus hanging there, the centurion said it for all of us: "Truly this man was God's Son!"

Could it be that this was the centurion's way of saying that Jesus was so good, so authentic, so genuine . . . he must be TRUE? He was God's man, God's son, God's Word become flesh. God's idea lived out. He was TRUE to what God meant life to be.

Isn't it interesting that even at the place of death, Jesus shows us how to live. Even as he dies, he reveals the most authentic qualities of life. Let me suggest a few of these qualities which emerge so graphically from the cross that they must be true, they must be of God.

FIRST, THERE IS LOVE. Love is so good, so beautiful, so fulfilling, so right that it must be true. Jesus believed that. He went to the cross for it. The quality of love is so special that it must be true life as God meant it to be.

Some years ago when our children were young, I saw our daughter do something nice and thoughtful for her brother. That simple act of kindness made me feel great joy, and I thought to myself: *There is nothing that makes me happier than to see our children loving each other, helping each other, caring for each other.*

Of course, sometimes they would annoy each other, and that always bothered me. That's a parable for life, isn't it? I'm sure there is nothing that makes God happier than to see us (his children) loving each other.

I'm equally sure that when we hurt each other, it breaks God's heart because God made us out of love and for love. Love is so good that it must be true life as God meant it to be. If you doubt that, then consider the alternatives—hate, cruelty, hostility, indifference. No, these are all false; all are fake. These are all distortions of God's plan and God's truth. The truth is that God made us for love.

SECOND, THERE IS HUMILITY. There is something very special, very God-like, about the spirit of humility.

While visiting in China, one of our Christian leaders asked a group of Chinese pastors what it was in Christ that appealed most to them and won their hearts to him. None of them mentioned the miracles or even the Sermon on the Mount. One of the elders in a choking, faltering voice told the story of the Upper Room—Christ taking a towel and washing the disciples' feet. He became a humble servant.

Humility is so good that it must be life as God meant it to be. If you doubt that, then consider the alternatives—pompous pride, self-centered arrogance, egotistical acts, our shabby ways of scrambling for the chief seats. No, all of these are false, fake, phony. All are distortions of God's will for our lives. The truth is that God made us for love and humility.

THIRD, THERE IS FORGIVENESS. Forgiveness is another quality of spirit that is so special, so big, that it must be true. Look at Jesus on the cross and hear him saying: "Father, forgive them!" That is so good that it has to be authentic, it has to be of God.

So, if you ever wonder, *Should I forgive that person who has wronged me or hurt me?*—if that question ever comes to your mind—then just remember the picture of Jesus hanging on a cross saying, "Father, forgive them."

That is our measuring stick for forgiveness. That is the way God wants us to be. If you doubt that, then consider the alternatives—resentment, bitterness, vengeance. No, these are all false. All are distortions of God's will for our lives. The truth is that God made us for love, humility, and forgiveness. God showed us that on a cross!

CHAPTER 16

ARE YOU TRAPPED BY YOUR FEARS?

MATTHEW 25:14-30

It was in the late 1960s. It occurred in a small Southern town. A middle-aged woman became desperately frightened. She was morbidly afraid that burglars or robbers would come and break into her home.

Maybe it was because of too much violence on television. Maybe it was because of newspaper reports on increases in the crime rate. Maybe it was because of rumors around town of numerous break-ins. Or, maybe it was a combination of these.

Whatever the case, she became increasingly frightened. Her fears mushroomed to paranoia.

She began to plead with her husband to put heavy bars on all the windows and doors of their home. Hoping to ease her mind, he finally agreed and had jail-like bars attached securely to all the windows and doors.

Still she was dissatisfied. Still she was frightened. So she talked her husband into adding additional strands of steel over the window bars, making it virtually impossible for anyone to gain entry to the house.

Now she was virtually sealed off from the outside world. She felt safer, much more secure. But there was one thing she didn't count on.

One afternoon as she was taking a nap, the house caught on fire. She awakened to find herself trapped in her bedroom. Her husband, firefighters, police officers, the emergency squad, and neighbors all worked frantically trying to get her out of the house but to no avail.

They could not bend the heavy window bars or break the strands of steel or remove them in time. Tragically, she lost her life—trapped by her own fears and trapped in a prison of her own making.

Isn't this a graphic parable for life? It seems to me that one of the great problems of life is dramatically encapsulated in this sad but true story.

People do get trapped and paralyzed by their fears. This is one of the real spiritual calamities of life—that some people who want so much to live a full, exciting, and zestful life get trapped in a prison of their own making.

They become imprisoned by their own fears. They want to get involved in the real issues and concerns. They want to make significant decisions and meaningful commitments. They want to count for something, but their fears paralyze them. This is precisely what happened to the one-talent servant in Jesus' parable of the talents. Obviously, he didn't have as much as the other two servants, but he had enough to do something good and productive. The problem was that he was afraid and his fears did him in. His fears trapped him, enslaved him, paralyzed him, and he just quit, threw in the towel, gave up, and did nothing. That's what fear does to us. It imprisons us.

Some people are trapped by the fear of commitment. Others are paralyzed by their fear of rejection, still others by their fear of failure. Some are immobilized by their fear of involvement, and as strange as it may sound, some persons are tied in knots by their fear of God.

Jesus realized this and he spent a lot of his time trying to set people free from their fears. Often when he would call people to a commitment to follow him, he would begin by telling them not to be afraid.

"Fear not," he would say. "Don't be anxious! Don't be afraid!"

What he was saying to them and to us is this, Don't be trapped or imprisoned by your own fears!

✦✦

CHAPTER 17

THIS IS MY MOMENT

MARK 10:17-22

I n the hit Broadway musical *Stop the World—I Want to Get Off!* Anthony Newley played a kind of everyman character named Little Chap and sang that powerful song "Once in a Lifetime," which has these poignant words: "This is my moment. . . . Just once in a lifetime, I'm gonna do great things."

"This is my moment." We have all known that feeling, haven't we? That special moment when something stirs within us and we know that a unique opportunity is now available to us, maybe never to return again in just this way.

We know the feeling of the crucial moment. But sadly, we must confess that we also know the empty feeling of missing our moment, of letting the moment pass.

The truth is that life is a series of crucial moments, decisive moments, or moments of decision. We all have sensed that this "now" is a special, crucial moment and I should say something or do something.

But because of fear or timidity or insecurity, we hesitate and let the moment slip by. We do nothing and we miss our moment and then we regret it greatly because we know deep down that we cannot reclaim it; that this special moment is gone forever.

There is an interesting psychological point here. Psychologists tell us that every time we have this kind of feeling, if we do not act on it, then we are less likely to act later when other such moments present themselves. Each time we fail to act, we become more closed, more withdrawn, more emotionally paralyzed.

A dramatic example of this is the schizophrenic patient sitting on the floor, leaning against the wall, crouched in the fetal position, not speaking to anyone or paying attention to anyone or anything. He is closed in, withdrawn, tuned out.

Now, of course, most of us don't go that far, but what we do is also paralyzing. We trick ourselves by substituting the emotion for the action. Let me repeat that. We substitute the emotion for the action.

For example, we feel something like sympathy or appreciation or a moral commitment and then in effect we say, "Well, that takes care of that!" And we do nothing. We trick ourselves into thinking that just because we felt it, it is cared for; that because we felt it, we have done it.

How many letters have never been written? How many phone calls have never been made? How many thank-yous do we never get around to? How many I love yous are still unexpressed? How many commitments are still not made because we missed our moment?

If we put it off, the moment passes, the feeling subsides and never gets done. We see this vividly in Scripture. The rich young ruler missed his moment.

Remember the crucial encounter? He is inspired by Jesus. Something stirs within him. Deep down he knows that Jesus is right, that Jesus has the answer to his emptiness. He knows that he should act, he feels it. But he turns away sorrowfully.

This story is a powerful portrait of the tragedy of the unseized moment. The rich young ruler missed it. He was a good man, the story makes that clear, but he let this unique opportunity slip through his fingers. Well, the real truth is that he is not alone.

In fact, most all of the tragic characters of the New Testament were people who missed their moment: Pontius Pilate, the elder brother, the priest and Levite, the one-talent servant, the foolish maidens, Judas Iscariot, just to mention a few. All graphically depict the tragedy of the unseized moment.

To bring this closer to home, look at the following unseized moments that can rise up to haunt us and fill us with regret.

1. First, there is the unseized moment of *caring*, that special opportunity when we might touch another person with love, help, kindness, or tenderness, only to let the moment pass, to look the other way, to put it off until tomorrow, to rationalize it, to pass by on the other side like the priest and Levite.

2. Second, there is the unseized moment of *reconciliation*, that moment when just a word or a touch could bring oneness and harmony, but instead we let pride or fear of rejection or jealousy stop it like the elder brother.

3. Third, there is the unseized moment of *opportunity*, that unique moment when we have a chance to do something

special or significant, only to let it slip through our fingers because of timidity or fear or insecurity or insensitivity like the one-talent servant.

4. Fourth, there is the unseized moment of *listening*, that urgent moment when a person needs to talk—and we miss it.

5. Fifth, there is the unseized moment of *appreciation*. How I have failed here—I need to write hundreds of letters. I need to make hundreds of phone calls or visits just to say thank you to people to whom I owe so much—teachers, pastors, neighbors, coworkers, relatives, counselors, friends who have made great sacrifices that have touched my life.

6. Sixth, there is the unseized moment of *commitment*, that moment when something stirs deep down in our souls and we know that we need to act, to make a new confession of loyalty, a new commitment, only to put it off, shrug it off, fight it off, and walk away sorrowfully like the rich young ruler.

May God help us be more aware and more sensitive and more willing to seize the great moments of life.

✦✦✦✦✦✦✦✦✦✦✦✦✦✦✦✦✦✦✦✦✦✦✦✦✦✦✦✦✦✦✦✦✦

CHAPTER 18

RESILIENCE: THE STRENGTH TO BEND WITHOUT BREAKING

MARK 15:1-15

One of Aesop's Fables tells of a mighty Oak Tree and a humble Reed growing side by side on the edge of a river. From time to time they spoke to each other, but they were not close friends because the mighty Oak looked down on the humble Reed.

"You have no pride," the Oak told the Reed. "You bend and bow to the lightest breeze. You should be more dignified and proud like me. You should stand erect as I do. No wind can make me stoop or lower myself."

Just then a fierce storm sprang up. Lightning flashed and strong winds blew hard and shook the trees. The unbending Oak stood firm for a short while. But his very stiffness was his undoing.

The storm struck hard against the Oak, tore his branches, broke his biggest boughs, and toppled him into the river.

Meanwhile the Reed swayed and bent, letting the wind blow over him, but he did not break. When the storm passed, he sprang back and was still growing on the edge of the river.

Now in this ancient fable, we see portrayed in a graphic way a valuable Christian quality. It is resilience: the strength to bend without breaking.

Resilience. What does it mean? Well, it's a big word for a big spirit. The dictionary defines resilience as the ability to spring back, the strength to bounce back, to return to the original form or position after being bent or compressed.

Resilience means buoyancy, the ability to recover readily from illness, depression, or adversity. It is not weakness, but instead it is strength to withstand shock without permanent damage.

To clarify it further, let me tell you what resilience is not.

It is not brittleness.

It is the opposite of self-pity.

It is the opposite of intolerance and closed-mindedness.

It is the opposite of legalism and a "holier than thou" attitude.

It is the opposite of resentment and bitterness.

Resilience means openness. It is the strength to bend without breaking. Psychologists are writing a great deal today about mental health and emphasizing the need for a resilience of spirit that will bend as a reed bends with the wind, but not break.

Self-improvement lecturer and writer Dale Carnegie once pointed out that the makers of automobile tires tried at first to make a tire that would resist the shocks of the road. It was a tire that was soon cut to pieces, torn to shreds. Then they started making tires that would give a little and absorb the shocks. Those tires are still with us. They are enduring because they are resilient; they give, they absorb, and they bounce back.

Similarly, we need to learn how to take the storms of life with resilience and not with resentment or self-pity.

The storms do come, the winds do blow, the rains do fall and the quality of resilience can serve us well in the living of these days. Let me show you what I mean:

1. We can be resilient when disappointments come. Disappointment is a fact of life. As J. Wallace Hamilton once said, "Every man's life is a diary in which he means to write one story and is forced to write yet another." Resilient people bounce back and turn their disappointments into victories.

2. We can be resilient in our service. Our calling is to serve God with all we have, wherever we may be. We can't always choose our place of serving. We can't all be chairpersons or presidents or bishops or governors or soloists. There are no perfect situations for serving anyway, so forget that— bounce back and love God and serve him wherever you are.

3. We can be resilient in our thinking. Most of us need help here. It is so easy to be brittle, hard, closes-minded, and unbending in our thinking. We need to remember that the mind is like a parachute; it works best when open.

4. We can be resilient in our relations with others. Resilience is one of the faces of love; it's the ability to give in and not always demand our way. It's the strength of understanding and com-passion and forgiveness—and we could all use a lot of that!

✦✦✦✦✦✦✦✦✦✦✦✦✦✦✦✦✦✦✦✦✦✦✦✦✦✦✦✦✦✦✦

CHAPTER 19

WHEN TROUBLE COMES

PSALM 23

The beautiful young woman sitting across the desk from me was deeply troubled. It was obvious. She was nervous, scared, grief-stricken, and heartbroken.

Understandably so, because just a few weeks before, a tragic farm accident had made her a widow in a matter of seconds. She was now a twenty-six-year-old widow with three preschool children.

Her bright, energetic young husband had been so strong, so prosperous, so active, so full of life; but then one morning his tractor had brushed against a hot electric wire and, that quickly, he was gone.

One minute alive, vibrant, full of love and vitality and fun, with great hopes and dreams for his future and for his family. The next minute gone.

Tears glistened in her eyes as she told me about him and his fatal accident. Her mascara smudged her cheeks just a bit from her constant and anxious dabbing at the corners of her eyes with a dainty handkerchief. The knuckles of her hands were white as she nervously twisted the handkerchief in her lap.

"I don't know how I am going to make it without him," she said, "but I know one thing: I have a choice to make. I can get bitter or I can get better. I have come to the church because I want to get better."

At that time, I had never heard it put that way before, but she had underscored a universal truth in a crystal clear way—when trouble comes, when life tumbles in around you, when disappointment breaks your heart, when sorrow grips your spirit, you have a choice. You can get bitter or you can get better.

Ralph Sockman once expressed it like this: "A grief is a sorrow we carry in our heart; a grievance is a chip we carry on our shoulder."

All of us at one time or another have to face trouble. It is universal and impartial, and none of us are immune.

There is no wall high enough to shut out trouble. There is no life, no matter how much it may be sheltered, that can escape from it. There is no trick, no matter how clever, by which to evade it.

Sometime, somewhere, and maybe even when we least expect it, trouble will rear its head, thrust its way into our lives, and confront and challenge each of us. The psalmist did not say: "I will meet no evil." He said: "I will fear no evil."

So, the question is not: *Will trouble come to me?* It will. Rather, the question is: *How do I respond to troubled waters?* The choice is mine and the option is clear. *Will I let this trouble make me bitter, or will I use it with God's help to get better?*

The psalmist said: "So teach us to number our days that we may get a heart of wisdom" (Psalm 90:12, paraphrased). This is just another way of saying, "Lord, teach us how to use every day to grow better—not bitter, but better."

This is the option before us when we run up against the troublesome experiences of life.

When disappointment comes, we can get bitter or better. When heartache comes, we can get bitter or better. When rejection comes, we can get bitter or better. When old age, physical illness, failure, embarrassment, or sorrow come, the choice is clear: we can give in to bitterness or we can grow on our troubles into bigger and better persons.

In dealing with personal tragedy, Aldous Huxley's words are true: "Experience is not what happens to you; it is what you do with what happens to you." That is what really matters.

CHAPTER 20

THE TRUTH WILL SET YOU FREE

JOHN 8:28-32

It was the summer of 1975. Cynthia was twenty-four years old. She had just graduated from the University of Texas at Austin when she saw a blind advertisement in the newspaper which read: "Sincere, conscientious person interested in the betterment of mankind: call this number . . ." Out of curiosity, Cynthia picked up the telephone and dialed the number. Little did she know that with that phone call, her mind had begun a journey from which it might never return. Before she realized what was happening to her in the next few days, she had become caught up in a radical youth movement and through the use of various subtle mind-manipulating techniques (some would later call it a brainwashing process), she was transformed into a kind of obedient, subservient zombie, doing whatever the group commanded without question. She was taught or programmed to believe that God was throwing Christianity away and replacing it with this radical new youth movement. She was told to forget her family, to forget her friends, to forget her past. Cynthia stayed with the group for a couple of months. At one point, she said, "I felt that someone had placed a psychological bomb on my head, and if I left the group it would explode." Toward the end of the summer, Cynthia had to return home to handle some unfinished personal business. The day after she arrived, she was eating breakfast when the doorbell rang. A man entered the room and introduced himself as a minister. Cynthia didn't know it at the time, but her parents had brought the minister in to "de-program" her.

Cynthia and the minister argued and debated and yelled at each other for eight hours. He showed her documents that exposed the youth movement and its dangers. He played her tapes of other young people who had been de-programmed, but nothing got through—nothing penetrated her confused mind. Then the minister did something that broke through. He reached over, picked up a Bible, turned to the eighth chapter of John's Gospel, and quietly read to her these words of Jesus: "You will know the truth, and the truth will make you free." The truth will make you free . . . those words exploded into Cynthia's mind. She said it was as though a light had been suddenly turned on in the room, and a tremendous burden was lifted from her shoulders. For the first time in months, she felt free, really free! The months that followed were hard for Cynthia. She said it was like adjusting to another planet. She said it was like withdrawing from a drug. She said she had to learn to think all over again. During those difficult days, the one thing that kept her going was that verse of scripture: "You will know the truth, and the truth will make you free." I hope that not one of us will ever have to experience what Cynthia went through, but the point is that the truth of Christ can indeed set us free. The truth of Christ can set us free from those things that ensnare us, encumber us, or imprison us.

This is a dominant theme in the Scriptures:

+ Zacchaeus was set free from his greed and loneliness.
+ The woman at the well was set free from her sordid past.
+ The woman caught in adultery was set free from her moral dilemma.

I don't know what is locking you up right now. Maybe it's greed or selfishness, maybe it's pride or vanity, maybe it's resentment or jealousy, maybe it's fear or prejudice. But, I do know that Christ has the key and he can set you free. No matter what it is, the truth of Christ can set you free!

In one of his imaginative tales, Lewis Carroll writes about a lock that runs frantically around, rushing to and fro in a panic. "What's the matter?" someone asks. The lock answers, "I am seeking for someone to unlock me!" Aren't we all? We want somebody to unlock us, to set us free to live zestfully and to celebrate life, but somehow we feel like zombies programmed just to go through the motions, locked up and sealed off from real vibrant living. The good news of our faith is that the truth of Christ can set us free from anything that's imprisoning us because he comes to show two tremendously important things. He shows us what God is like and what God wants us to be like—and the word is "Love." Nothing is more freeing than that—to realize that God is loving and that God wants us to be loving. That truth sets us free!

++++++++++++++++++++++++++++++++++++

CHAPTER 21

WHY NOT YOU?

JOHN 21:15-19

A pastor in the Midwest had agreed to pinch-hit in the pulpit for a friend one Sunday morning. He went early to the church to see what it was like and to get the feel of the church's atmosphere.

As he was walking down a long hallway with his sermon notes in one hand and his pulpit robe draped over his other arm, he came upon a large room that was being used as a nursery for preschoolers.

When he glanced into the room, he saw a little boy who looked to be about four years old and who was all by himself in the nursery. The little boy said: "Hi, my name's Tommy and I'm all alone in this big room."

The visiting preacher had done a lot of counseling during his years in the ministry, so he decided to use his nondirective counseling technique on the little boy and he answered: "You feel all alone in that room?"

"I don't just feel it. I know I am all alone."

"Don't you worry now," the minister responded. "I'm sure that before too long somebody will come to be with you."

With wistful eyes, little Tommy looked up at him and said: "Why not you?"

"Why not you?" That's the question which resounds across the ages, and yet, more often than not, we ignore it, neglect it, fail to hear it, or refuse to act upon it. More often than not, we feel that surely someone else will come along and do what needs to be done.

- ✦ A problem needs to be solved.
- ✦ A word needs to be spoken.
- ✦ A job needs to be done.
- ✦ A situation needs to be corrected.
- ✦ A person needs to be helped.
- ✦ A church needs to be reformed.
- ✦ A community needs to be improved.
- ✦ A reconciliation needs to be worked.
- ✦ A word of appreciation needs to be expressed.
- ✦ A wrong needs to be righted.

We know it. We see it. We want these things to be done, but we expect somebody else to see to it. We feel that someone else more talented or more eloquent or more authoritative or more committed will come along and do what needs to be done.

But the question of God directed personally to each one of us is simply this: "Why not you?"

One of the most significant keys to successful and meaningful living is found here: to be able to see something that should be done and to take it on and do something about it.

When you stop and think about it, you see that the great people of faith in the Scriptures and down through history were those who saw a situation that needed to be made better and heard the call of God in that penetrating, personal question "Why not you? Why don't you correct this?" and then had the courage to take up the torch, to speak the word, to do the deed.

Just think of it. Moses, Isaiah, Jesus, Peter, Paul, Luther, Wesley, Mother Teresa—all of them and many more like them saw a problem and heard God calling them to do something about it. Each responded creatively and courageously to the question, "Why not you?"

The risen Christ on the seashore that morning was saying to Simon Peter, "If you love me, feed my sheep. If you love me, take up the torch of my ministry!" Or in other words, the risen Christ was saying to Peter, "Somebody needs to continue my ministry of love. Why not you?" And as we now know, Simon Peter heard the call that day. He saw the need and he responded with faith, trust, and obedience.

Let me suggest something. Every time you see a situation that needs correcting or a job that needs to be done or a person who needs to be helped, do you know what that means? It means that God is calling you to do something. If you see it, then that is God's way of calling you.

He is asking: "Why don't you do something about this? Why don't you right this wrong? Why don't you make this world a better place? Why not you?"

CHAPTER 22

KEEP ON KEEPING ON

HEBREWS 10:23-25

The middle-aged woman sitting across from me was crest-fallen. She was burdened, confused, heartbroken, and scared.

Her husband of more than twenty years had suddenly died three months before. Now the grief-pains of that loss were eating her up, gnawing away at her incessantly.

"I still cry a lot," she said to me, "especially late at night. I feel so alone, so afraid, so unable to cope, so disillusioned.

"When he died, it seems like a big part of me died with him. My whole world was wrapped up in him. And now he is gone. What in the world am I going to do? I have faith. I love God and I trust him, but where is he now when I need him so desperately? I know he is out there somewhere, but somehow I feel like I have been jolted out of contact with him."

I guess we all can identify with her and the agonizing despair in her words as she cries out for God. We have known painful moments like that. This is the way life feels sometimes.

We have faith, we believe. We try to live our faith daily. We trust God. But, despite that, there are moments in our lives when we seem to be out of touch with God, when faith is hard to hold on to, when God seems far away.

Those difficult moments come for all of us when we feel disillusioned, disappointed, and downhearted.

Now the questions are: How do we deal with disillusionment in a productive way? How do we handle disappointments creatively? How do we get "up" when we feel so downcast? How does a broken heart get mended? How do we keep the faith when it's hard?

One of my favorite people was Maida Mickle. She was a saint in the church. She was not a pious, puritanical, sanctimonious saint, but a "salty saint," full of life and vigor and wit and vibrancy. She had two favorite sayings that help us find an answer to disillusionment.

First, she said: "I would rather wear out than rust out!" And second, she said: "We have to keep on keeping on!"

In essence, this was what the writer of Hebrews was saying to the early Christians who were under heavy persecution. They were tired, scared, confused, and downhearted. The writer knew it and in Hebrews 10 he wrote these words: "Let us be firm and unswerving in the confession of our hope, for God can be trusted. So let us stir up one another to love, encouraging one another, and let us continue to meet together for worship" (author's paraphrase).

In other words, he was saying, "Don't quit! Don't give up! Don't lose heart! Keep on keeping on!" When you feel disillusioned and disappointed and downhearted, remember these words. They can lift your spirits; they can help put the stars back in the sky for you. Let me bring this closer with three quick thoughts.

1. WHEN YOU FEEL DISILLUSIONED, KEEP LOVING OTHERS. Read in different words how the writer of Hebrews put it: "Let us *stir up one another* to works of love and good deeds!"

He was so right. The best antidote for the poison of despair is to reach out and touch someone with love. The best way to get over your problem is to get outside yourself, to forget yourself into usefulness!

As we reach out to others with love, our disillusionment fades and is replaced by happiness and fulfillment. That's the way it is. Jesus put it like this: "When we lose ourselves for others, then we find ourselves" (author's paraphrase).

2. WHEN YOU FEEL DISAPPOINTED, KEEP ENCOUR-AGING OTHERS. The writer of Hebrews reminds us that we are a family, a community of faith sharing the joys and sorrows of life together from the cradle to the grave.

"Encourage one another," he says to us. We were never meant to bear our burdens by ourselves. It is the genius of Christian faith that it recognizes this truth.

You see, we solve our problems better in community than in isolation. We all need a support group, a support system to affirm us, to uphold us, to encourage us, and that is a significant part of the task of the church.

One of the great personalities of the early church was Barnabas. That's a great name because it means "son of encouragement" and that is precisely what Barnabas was—an encourager. May God help each of us to be a "modern-day Barnabas"—someone who listens, who cares, who affirms, who lifts up, who helps others.

If you feel disappointed, the best way to get over it is to keep on keeping on—and to keep on encouraging others.

3. WHEN YOU FEEL DOWNHEARTED, KEEP TRUSTING GOD AND WORSHIPING HIM. Remember how the writer of Hebrews put it: "Don't neglect meeting together!"

Worship was what he was talking about, and he was right. When we get discouraged or feel defeated, we need to get into the presence of God. Worship is our great reminder that God is the Lord of life and that God is on our side, that he is with us and he will see us through, that nothing, not even death, can separate us from him.

So, when times are hard, keep on keeping on! Keep on loving others and keep on encouraging others and keep on trusting God.

◆◆◆◆◆◆◆◆◆◆◆◆◆◆◆◆◆◆◆◆◆◆◆◆◆◆◆◆◆◆◆◆◆◆◆◆

CHAPTER 23

WHEN CRISIS COMES

MATTHEW 25:1-13

Some years ago, a man came to my office. He was deeply troubled. He said: "Jim, I need to talk. I feel so empty, so dried up inside. I'm scared and lonely."

He paused for a moment, looked at the floor, and then he continued.

"I have just come from my doctor's office. He told me that I have a terminal illness. I have six months, maybe a year to live. As that news sunk in, I realized that I have no spiritual resources, no spiritual strength to face this. I have nothing to fall back on, nothing to lean on. Some people think I'm wealthy and materially I am, but that doesn't matter now, does it? Really and truly, I'm poor in the things that count most. I have all these years put my faith in the wrong things. The truth is: I am spiritually destitute!"

He paused again and then, as if he were thinking out loud, he said:

"You know, I could pick up that telephone and call any bank and borrow any amount of money to do whatever I wanted. Just on my name, I could borrow . . ."

His voice trailed off; he leaned over and put his head in his hands and very quietly he whispered:

"I guess there are some things you just can't borrow!"

As he spoke, I was reminded of a parable that Jesus once told that underscores this truth: when crisis comes, there are some things you cannot borrow. The story, which is found in the twenty-fifth chapter of Matthew, is about an incident at a wedding celebration called the parable of the wise and foolish maidens or the parable on preparedness.

In the parable, the neighborhood girls are waiting for the crucial moment, the exciting moment when the groom takes his bride to their new home. There is a long delay and the girls fall asleep. But then at midnight there is a shout and the girls awake. It's the announcement that the big moment is near—the bride and groom will be coming out very shortly.

According to the story, some of the young girls (the foolish ones) had not anticipated the long wait and had not prepared well enough in advance and now the moment is upon them and they have run short of oil for their lamps. They hastily try to borrow some, but cannot, so they rush off to get more oil, only to find on their return that the moment has passed, the celebration is over, and they missed out because they were not adequately prepared.

The point is clear: when crisis comes, you better have prepared ahead, because there are some things you can't borrow. When the crucial moments come, you have to take responsibility for your own life. It's good to have borrowing power; it's good to have material wealth; it's good to have friends to lean on; but sometimes you have to stand alone—you have to stand on your own two feet.

The businessman who came to my office that day had learned it the hard way. Jesus had taught it long ago: when crisis comes, there are some things you just cannot borrow. Here are a few examples.

FIRST, WHEN CRISIS COMES, YOU CANNOT BORROW A SPIRIT OF INNER POISE. The sense of poise, confidence, balance, control, stability . . . you can't borrow that. It has to be cultivated and grown, and then when crisis comes, it serves you well. Spiritual poise does not come instantly; it comes only from spending time with God.

It is quite simply the confidence, the "blessed assurance" that God is with us in every circumstance of life and even beyond and that nothing—not even death—can separate us from him and his love. So, we don't have to run scared or be afraid. We can be poised because God is with us and he loves us as a Father. But you can't borrow spiritual poise. You have to grow your own.

SECOND, WHEN CRISIS COMES YOU CAN'T BORROW THE BIBLE. Of course, you could borrow someone's copy of the Bible, but in a crisis you need your own Bible; you need the Scriptures written indelibly on your heart, and that doesn't happen overnight.

In desperation, people sometimes turn to the Bible for strength and comfort, and sometimes they come up empty, because they don't know how to find its treasures. The Bible becomes the Word of God for us not when we grab it up looking for easy answers and quick solutions, but rather after long exposure to its contents when it gets hold of us and inside of us!

THIRD, WHEN CRISIS COMES YOU CAN'T BORROW A PRAYER LIFE. It's good to have others praying for us, but we also need our own prayer life. In fact, I have learned in my own life that when I have difficulty praying it is a warning signal to me that I may be drifting away from the faith. A good prayer life is something we all need, and it is something we can't borrow.

FOURTH, WHEN CRISIS COMES YOU CAN'T BORROW THE CHURCH. Now, of course, people do borrow the church building for weddings and funerals and meetings. We offer it gladly, but there is something very sad to me about people who, having no church, come to borrow one, for all they can borrow is a physical structure. They can't really borrow the church because what makes the church really the church can't be loaned out.

FINALLY, WHEN CRISIS COMES YOU CAN'T BORROW A PERSONAL FAITH COMMITMENT. Each of us must find his or her own faith. As an unknown fifteenth-century poet put it:

> Thou shalt know Him when He comes.
> Not by any din of drums,
> Nor by the vantage of His airs,
> Nor by anything He wears,
> Neither by His crown,
> Nor by His gown.
> For His Presence known shall be
> By the Holy Harmony
> Which His coming makes in thee!

Do you know that holy harmony? You can't borrow that. It only comes from a personal encounter and relationship with the living Lord!

✦✦✦✦✦✦✦✦✦✦✦✦✦✦✦✦✦✦✦✦✦✦✦✦✦✦✦✦✦✦

CHAPTER 24

THE POWER OF WORDS

JOHN 1:1-18

Learning the right words—how important that is. What we say and how we say it reveals much about who we are and what we believe.

A friendly postman started a conversation with a four-year-old boy about his baby sister. "Can she talk?" the postman asked.

"No," the little boy answered. "She has her teeth, but her words haven't come in yet." This is an important part of the growing-up process—getting our words in, getting the right words in.

The right words can bring peace; the wrong words can cause war. The right words can bring harmony; the wrong words can cause discord. The right words can bring healing; the wrong words can cause pain. The right words can produce love; the wrong words can spread hatred.

Words are so important, so powerful, so influential. A word can excite you. A word can depress you. A word can make you glad or sad or mad. Words can inspire you to stand firm for what is right and good and true or they can destroy hope, blast reputations, and take the wind out of your sails.

It's important to learn the right words, the words of life, words that are creative and not destructive. Isn't that what we are about in the church, in our schools, in our homes? We are trying to learn the right words.

The point is made graphically in a legend from ancient Greece. Remember it? Xanthus is preparing for an important banquet. He orders his servant Aesop to provide the best things from the marketplace for his guests. When the guests arrive at the banquet table, they are surprised.

Each course consists of tongue with different sauces. When Xanthus complains, Aesop answers: "Nothing is better than tongue. It is the bond of civil society, the organ of truth and reason, the instrument of our praise to God."

The next day, out of curiosity, Xanthus orders Aesop to prepare a meal using the worst things from the marketplace. Aesop again surprises Xanthus and his guests. Each course again consists of tongue with different sauces.

Upon being reprimanded, Aesop answers: "The tongue is also the worst thing. It is lies, blasphemes, the source of division and war."

The point is clear, the tongue can be the best part of people or it can be the worst. Our words can encourage and motivate or they can crush and kill. How important it is that we learn the right words, like the following:

1. The words of kindness. We don't have to be rude or harsh or hateful or hostile. We can be kind. We can speak the words of kindness. In my opinion, one of the most important and impressive signs of faith is kindness. You can be an

authority in theology; you can speak of the great philosophers; you can master church history; you can quote verses of scripture. But, only when you show kindness do people begin to see your faith.

2. The words of appreciation. We don't have to be thoughtless. We don't have to take things or people for granted. We can be grateful. We can speak the sounds of thanksgiving. We can learn the words of appreciation by continually expressing thanks for specific things until it becomes a habit.

3. The words of love. Jesus is the measuring stick for the words of love. He spoke words of tenderness: "Come to me, all you that are weary and are carrying heavy burdens, and I will give you rest." He spoke words of peace: "Peace I leave with you, my peace I give to you." He spoke words of hope: "In my father's house are many dwelling places." He spoke words of forgiveness: "Father, forgive them." He spoke words of love: "I give you a new commandment, that you love one another. Just as I have loved you, you also should love one another."

Jesus constructively criticized the wrong and he strongly defended the right, but always there was love and mercy and when he spoke people heard and saw God and they called him "The Word."

This is our challenge to so speak that our words reflect kindness, appreciation, love, the spirit of God, to so speak that our words fill the air not with the sounds of hate and hostility, not with the sounds of vengeance or cruelty or self-pity, but rather with the words of life.

CHAPTER 25

SPIRITUAL CATARACTS

MATTHEW 6:19-24

Early this week I asked a friend in the medical profession to give me a good definition of a cataract. The description of a cataract given to me was even better and more helpful than I had expected it to be. Look at this definition and at the same time think about "spiritual cataracts."

In medical terms, a cataract is a clouding over of the crystalline lens of the eye or of its capsule. This filminess causes a loss of transparency and obstructs the passage of the waves of light into the eye. Because the rays of light entering the eye must pass through the pupil and lens to reach the retina, any cloudiness in the lens will cause distorted vision.

There is no pain; the loss of vision is gradual; it slips up on you.

The cataract abnormality may occur in younger individuals as a result of some trauma but most commonly occurs in adults.

If left unattended, the cloudiness may become so heavy that no light can get through at all and vision is lost altogether. Cataracts can be removed by surgery.

Now this medical description brings to mind the words of Jesus in Matthew 6 as he says: "The eye is the lamp of the body. If your eye is sound, your whole body will be full of light; but if your eye is not sound your whole body will be full of darkness" (author's paraphrase).

Jesus is suggesting here that we need to beware of "spiritual cataracts"—beware of things that cloud and distort our vision.

The idea behind this passage in the Sermon on the Mount is one of childlike simplicity. The eye is regarded as the window by which the light gets into the whole body. The state of the window determines how much light gets into a room.

If the window is clear, clean, undistorted, then the light will come flooding into the room and will illuminate every corner of it.

However, if the glass of the window is colored or frosted, clouded or distorted, dirty or obscure, then the light will be hindered and obstructed and the room will not be lit up—but will be rather dark and gloomy.

The amount of light which gets into any room depends on the state of the window through which it has to pass. So, Jesus says that the light that gets into any person's heart and soul and being depends on the spiritual state of the eye through which it has to pass, for the eye is the window of the whole body.

It is interesting to note here that in the Greek language, which was the original language of the New Testament, the word "body" often meant more than the physical anatomy. It often meant what we in the twenty-first century would call the "total personality."

Think again about the Scripture lesson in light of that. It would read like this: "The eye is the lamp of the total personality." The way we see things, the way we look at things, the way we view things, the perspective we bring to things, it says a lot about our total personalities.

The way you view other people says a lot about your spiritual life.

The way you view your job says a lot about your spiritual life.

The way you view material things says a lot about your spiritual life.

The way you view the world says a lot about your spiritual life.

The way you view life says a lot about your spiritual life.

On an old *Andy Griffith Show* on television, deputy Barney Fife has sent off for an amateur psychiatry kit. When it arrives, he decides to try it out on Otis, the town drunk. Barney takes the ink blot test over to Otis and asks, "What do you see?" Otis says, "I see a bat!" Barney gets upset and says to Otis, "That's the difference between you and me, Otis. You see a bat and I see a butterfly."

Barney is precisely on target—the difference between people is often most clearly demonstrated by the way we see things.

When Jesus implies that we beware of "spiritual cataracts," he is reminding us that there are certain obvious things that can blind our eyes and distort our vision. Prejudice, narrowness, jealousy, fear, despair, selfishness—these are the spiritual cataracts of life.

CHAPTER 26

CUT IT OFF— THROW IT AWAY? DID JESUS REALLY MEAN THAT?

MATTHEW 5:29-30

Some years ago when I was in seminary at the Methodist Theological School in Ohio, I was assigned one spring semester to be a student chaplain at the Riverside Methodist Hospital in Columbus, Ohio.

I had a number of fascinating experiences in that clinical training experience. One of them came into my mind recently. It was the day the head chaplain invited all the student chaplains to come in early to watch surgery being performed.

We first witnessed an appendectomy. It was not easy to watch the surgeon's knife cut into living flesh, and some in our group wilted and almost fainted. Some, feeling squeamish, had to leave the room.

I made it all right through the appendectomy and another minor surgical procedure. But then they made preparations to amputate a young man's leg. I recoiled at that. I turned white, felt faint, and had to leave the room.

As I hurriedly left, I found myself wanting to stop the doctors, to stop the whole proceeding. Amputation, cutting off a limb, seemed so horribly final and I found myself nauseated by the thought.

It is probably this same kind of inner revulsion that makes us flinch and draw back from this strange-sounding, disturbing command of Jesus in the Sermon on the Mount. Listen again to his shocking words: "If your right eye causes you to sin, tear it out and throw it away. . . . And if your right hand causes you to sin, cut it off and throw it away; it is better for you to lose one of your members than for your whole body to go into hell."

Tear it out? Cut it off? Did Jesus say that? Is this the "gentle Jesus meek and mild" that we sing about? Is this the personable Jesus who took little children into his arms and blessed them? Is this the sensitive Jesus who loved the birds of the air and the flowers of the field? Is this the compassionate Jesus who touched the man with the withered hand and made him whole?

What are we to make of this? These words sound so harsh, so stark, so brutal. "Tear it out . . . cut it off . . . throw it away." There must be some truth here that is tremendously important to prompt Jesus to speak so strongly and so unflinchingly! Let's see if we can uncover it. Here are three ideas to try on for size.

FIRST, JESUS IS SPEAKING SYMBOLICALLY. The actual cutting off of a hand or a foot and the literal plucking out of an eye were not what Jesus had in mind. He is speaking dramatically here, to be sure, but he is speaking symbolically.

He did this a lot. Roy Pearson, in his book *The Hard Commands of Jesus*, said it well: "Jesus said that his disciples were 'the salt of the Earth,' but no one thought he meant that they should be used as seasoning on meat. He called them, 'the light of the world,' but no one tried to use them as lamps for his home. And when Jesus spoke of plucking out the offending eye and cutting off the tempting hand, he did not have in mind an act involving knives and gouges."

Jesus is speaking symbolically, calling us to the discovery of a much deeper truth, namely, that anything destructive, anything threatening to destroy us, any one part threatening the existence of the whole must be radically cut out of our lives before it contaminates and ruins us.

SECOND ALTHOUGH IT MAY SOUND HARSH, THE TRUTH IS THAT WE DO, AS A MATTER OF FACT, OPERATE ON THIS "CUT IT OFF—GET RID OF IT" PRINCIPLE ALL THE TIME. Ask any doctor. If you have an appendix about to rupture and spread its poison, the doctor will not hesitate to cut it out. If skin cancer appears on your finger and threatens to get into the blood stream, the doctor will say, "Let's get rid of it!" The whole body is more important than any one of its dispensable parts.

Ask any dentist about this principle. He will tell you that there are times when you are better off to have that abscessed tooth pulled out before its terrible infection does harm that cannot be repaired.

Ask any athlete about the things that have to be cut out of his or her life before he or she can be honed into a finely tuned perfect athletic condition. No smoking, no alcohol, no late hours, no laziness, and certain foods must be left out and cut off.

Ask any scientist. This principle is the basis of the scientific method. You experiment and if it doesn't work, you throw it out. It if doesn't prove true, you get rid of it.

Or ask any parent. One of my mother's favorite lines to my brother and me when as children we got too loud or too quiet was, "Boys, whatever you are doing in there—Cut it out!"

THIRD, NOWHERE IS THIS "CUT IT OUT" PRINCIPLE TRUER THAN IN THE SPIRITUAL DIMENSIONS OF OUR PERSONAL LIVES. There are certain acts, attitudes, habits, or sins that will contaminate, infect, and poison our souls.

Envy, jealousy, resentment, greed, hate, arrogance, selfishness—these are spiritual cancers! The only way we can be spiritually well is to get rid of them, cut them out. We must amputate these things. Nothing less than radical surgery will do!

Scottish evangelist Henry Drummond was right when he said that most of the difficulties of trying to live the Christian life come from attempting to half live it.

What about you? Be honest. In your spiritual life, do you need radical surgery?

✦✦✦✦✦✦✦✦✦✦✦✦✦✦✦✦✦✦✦✦✦✦✦✦✦✦✦✦✦✦✦✦✦✦✦✦

CHAPTER 27

ONE STEP AT A TIME

MATTHEW 6:25-34

It is interesting to note that poets, hymn writers, and theologians have often referred to our faith as a walk, a Christian walk, a walk with God.

Perhaps that is a good analogy because we know that walking is something we do one step at a time and this "one-step-at-a-time" formula may well be one of the most significant keys to mastering life.

This principle for living is captured in some lines from one of the most popular hymns of all time, "Lead, Kindly Light." Remember the words:

"Keep Thou my feet, I do not ask to see the distant scene; one step enough for me."

Do you remember Thomas Carlyle? There was a period in his life when he was living in almost total poverty and defeat. During this time he labored for many, many long hours to write the first volume of the history of the French Revolution. It was his greatest work and he felt that it could and would bring to him the literary success he sought and deserved.

Finally the first volume was completed. Carlyle was excited and pleased. He took it to his friend John Stuart Mill to read and critique. Mill sat by the fire in his home and carefully read the remarkable work page by page, and he was greatly impressed by Carlyle's work.

But then one morning the maid was cleaning the room and seeing the disarrayed pages of the manuscript on the floor by John Stuart Mill's chair, she thought they were just trash; she thought they were just papers he had discarded. So, she used them to build a fire.

All that work, all that research, all those hours of struggle were quickly burned away. In a scant few seconds, it had all gone up in smoke.

When Thomas Carlyle learned that the work into which he had put so much was destroyed, he was devastated. He became a deeply depressed and defeated man. He had neither the strength nor the heart to start over. In bitterness, he vowed that he would never write again. For days and days, he brooded over his misfortune and gave way to self-pity.

Then, one day he looked out his window and saw a man building a brick wall. He watched as the man picked up one brick at a time and set it in place. He was building that large wall, one brick at a time.

As Thomas Carlyle watched, he decided he would write his book again, by writing one page at a time. He did just that and it became a classic, and he became one of the greatest writers and lecturers of Victorian England.

One step at a time. It was a major breakthrough for Thomas Carlyle and it can be so for you and me.

After all, it would have been strange of God to make a world that would prove to be too much for his children. It would have been thoughtless and cruel of him to make a world with burdens too heavy for human shoulders to bear. I don't believe God made that mistake.

Now, let's admit it. Some people do collapse under the pressures, but many of these persons come apart from the strain because they have not learned how to take life one day at a time, one step at a time.

This seems to be the way God meant for us to live because we see this principle in Jesus' life and words. Jesus taught us to pray, "Give us THIS day our daily bread." THIS day's bread is all we ever really need, and this day, *today*, is the only day of which we are sure.

But how easy it is to forget that and pass over this day and spend our energies in anxious concern over bread for tomorrow and the day after. Jesus said to take it one step at a time. "Give us THIS day our daily bread."

Also, in the Sermon on the Mount, Jesus said, "Do not be anxious about tomorrow, for tomorrow will be anxious for itself. Let today's own trouble be sufficient for today" (author's paraphrase). That is, take each day as it comes . . . step by step . . . and one step at a time.

✦✦✦✦✦✦✦✦✦✦✦✦✦✦✦✦✦✦✦✦✦✦✦✦✦✦✦✦✦✦✦✦✦✦

CHAPTER 28

ARE YOU REALLY COMMITTED?

MATTHEW 6:13-20

A young man in his mid-twenties walked into our church recently. He looked tired, worried, burdened. He was slumped over as if carrying a heavy load on his back.

"What's the matter?" I asked. "You look like you are carrying all the troubles of the world on your shoulders."

"No," he said sadly, "not all the troubles. The truth is I just have one problem. My problem is that I am not really committed to anything."

What about you? Could that be your problem? Are you totally committed, unconditionally committed to anyone or to anything?

It does seem that we are living in a time when people are reluctant to make commitments; and when they do make them they are often tentative, cautious, measured—with lots of loopholes.

In his book *What About Tomorrow?* J. Wallace Hamilton suggests that commitment, like the Old Gray Mare, "just ain't what she used to be." The following are his words:

This age of ours is full of fleeing people, people who are unconsciously running out on life. . . . There has grown up in our time an almost pathological desire to escape from the difficulties, the drudgeries and even the realities of life. . . . If you like it, you live with it. If you don't like it, you leave it. It is amazing how much that spirit of irresponsibility (that lack of real commitment) is in the very marrow of this age.

Think with me about that for a moment.

1. We see it in the growing number of marriage breakdowns. People going into marriage, one foot in and one foot out . . . and then bailing out when the going gets rough.

2. We see it in the "runaway syndrome." Runaway teenagers, runaway fathers, and now even an increasing number of runaway moms.

3. We see it in our escapism crutches. When problems arise or troubles come, literally millions of people try to hide behind tranquilizers, alcohol, or hard drugs.

4. We see it in an increase in the emotional problem we call the "blahs"; the housekeeping blues, the child-raising depressions, the school-day hangover, the "no-date Friday night lonelies," the office boredoms, and a host of other current-day pressures that drain us emotionally and spiritually and make people want to flee from their responsibilities and commitments rather than to stand firm.

5. We see it, too, in the work world. Who wants to work these days? Hard work, sacrifice, the discipline of toil. Who wants that? Too many have fallen for the lie that we can get something for nothing, that we can get wages without work, that

we can win without struggle or discipline or sweat, that we can have a good world without working to make it good.

6. Then, what about our commitment to God and his church? How would you rate your commitment? Your faith commitment? Do you really put God first? Do you really love him with all your heart, soul, mind, and strength?

Do you really love your neighbor as much as you love yourself? Are you really committed to God's kingdom and to the doing of God's will? Are you really Christ-like in your style of living and relating to others? Are you really committed to support the church and uphold the church with your prayers, your presence, your gifts, and your service?

Or do you quit when the going gets rough? Or do you serve God and the church only when it's convenient? Or do you run out when things don't go just as you want them to?

Think about it. Are you really committed to God, to serving him and giving him first place no matter what—come what may? Total commitment—that's what we are talking about; commitment without conditions. It's the stuff that great people are made of.

It's Job, crying out in the midst of great pain, "Though he slay me, yet will I trust in Him!" (KJV). It's Nehemiah, facing criticism and hostility and threats and saying, "Should such a man as I flee?" (KJV).

It's Bonhoeffer praying in a Nazi prison camp: "Lord, whatever this day may bring . . . Your name be praised."

It's Luther, facing tremendous authoritative pressure, saying, "Here I stand: I can do no other!"

It's Patrick Henry shouting: "Give me liberty or give me death!"

It's Abraham Lincoln, after speaking on a controversial subject, saying, "If I go down because of this speech, then let me go down linked to the truth."

It's Susanna Wesley calling all her children to her deathbed and saying to them: "Now children as soon as I am released, sing a hymn of praise!"

It's John Bunyan (after being told that he would be released from prison if he would promise to stop preaching) saying, "I am determined yet to suffer till moss grows over my eyebrows rather than to violate my faith!"

It's Shadrach, Meshach, and Abednego—facing the heat of King Nebuchadnezzar's wrath and his fiery furnace—still being able to say, "O Nebuchadnezzar, we are not worried about what will happen to us. Our God is able to deliver us. But if not . . . even if he doesn't . . . we will never break our commitment to him. We will not bow down. We will worship God alone" (author's paraphrase).

Total commitment, commitment without conditions—commitment that can stand the heat—is our calling as Christian people. That is the spirit in which we are to live.

We must not—we dare not—lose the spirit of commitment. We must stand for something, lest we fall for everything!

✦✦✦✦✦✦✦✦✦✦✦✦✦✦✦✦✦✦✦✦✦✦✦✦✦✦✦✦✦✦✦✦✦✦

CHAPTER 29

THE POWER OF YOUR INFLUENCE

MATTHEW 5:13-16

A lbert Schweitzer was one of the great men of history. He was an intellectual giant, a physician, a prominent Christian theologian, an oft-quoted author, a superb organist, and the world's foremost authority on the music of Bach. Some would have said that Schweitzer had the world at his feet.

Do you know what he did? When he was thirty, he renounced the promise of a great and prosperous European career to give his life to the immediate service of others as a doctor in Africa's jungle. He spent forty years as a missionary.

Schweitzer built a hospital and a settlement on the Ogowe River in Africa with his own hands and paid for medical supplies by giving organ recitals in Vienna, London, and Paris. In his lifetime, he was a crusader for world peace and a winner of the Nobel Peace Prize.

He was one of the truly great men of our time. He died in 1965, but his philosophy, especially his ethical code of reverence for life, of protecting life, is still with us.

I have to admit that sometimes when I pick up a fly swatter at home and begin to stalk a fly, I think of Schweitzer and his reverence for life, and I put the fly swatter down and shoo the fly out of the house. Schweitzer has had a great and powerful Christian influence on the world.

I like what the influential editor and writer Norman Cousins said about him: "The greatness of Schweitzer—indeed, the essence of Schweitzer—was what others have done because of him and the power of his example. . . . This is the measure of the man." Isn't that a great quotation? It's not so much what he has done but what others have done because of him. Isn't that the real measure of every person? Not so much what we do, but it's what we cause others to do. It's what others do because of us.

It's the power of our example—the power of our influence. What kind of example are you? How do you influence other people? What do others do because of you?

Some years ago, a group in our country wanted to honor Schweitzer and they brought him to America.

The University of Chicago planned to honor him with an honorary degree. Dr. McGifford of the university went with a group to meet Schweitzer's train. They saw the great philosopher get off the train, greeted him, and told him of their joy in having him there.

All of a sudden Schweitzer was gone. He just disappeared. He had slipped away. They looked everywhere for him.

When they found him, guess what he was doing. He was carrying a suitcase for an older woman. You see, it was so much a part of his life, his Christ-inspired life, that it was just natural for him when he got off the train to begin immediately to look for somebody he could help.

But the thing I remember most about that story was what Dr. McGifford said later when he reflected on it. He said that when he saw Schweitzer helping that woman with her suitcase, he was wishing like everything that he could find somebody whose suitcase he could carry.

The power of influence—the power of example—it's not just what you do. It's what others do because of you. Schweitzer is an example of a Christian man who made those around him want to do good.

But, of course, the perfect example was Jesus. It wasn't just what he did; it was also what he caused others to do. Attributed to the Reverend James Francis is the classic piece that all of us have heard called "One Solitary Life." Hear it again.

> Here is a man who was born in an obscure village, the child of a peasant woman. He grew up in an obscure village. He worked in a carpenter shop until he was thirty and then for three years he was an itinerant teacher. He never wrote a book. He never held an office. He never ever owned a home. He never went to college. He never traveled, except in his infancy, more than two hundred miles from the place where he was born.
>
> He never did one of those things that usually accompany greatness. He had no credentials but himself. While he was still a young man, the tide of popular opinion turned against him. His friends ran away. One of them denied him. He was turned over to his enemies.

He went through the mockery of a trial. He was nailed upon a cross between two thieves. His executioners gambled for the only piece of property he had on earth—his seamless robe. He was laid to rest in a borrowed grave.

Nineteen centuries have come and gone, and today he is the centerpiece of the human race and the leader of all human progress.

I am well within the mark when I say that all the armies that ever marched, all the navies that ever were built, all the parliaments that ever sat, and all the kings that ever reigned, put together, have not affected the life of man upon this earth as powerfully as has this one solitary personality.

The power of influence—it was not just what he did, but it was also what others did because of him.

++

CHAPTER 30

MADE FOR THE SKIES AND CRAMMED IN A CAGE

ROMANS 12:1-2

The great British preacher W. E. Sangster tells of one day going to a zoo. As he was walking about, he came upon an eagle in a cage.

He stood there, looked at it, and saw powerful wings, beautifully feathered and meant for the skies and flying. As he stood looking at the eagle, someone in the crowd expressed his feelings, saying, "Made for the skies and crammed in a cage."

Think about that phrase for a moment. "Made for the skies and crammed in a cage." There is a powerful message there and it brings many different images to mind:

1. I think of the apostle Paul writing to the Roman Christians and saying, "Don't let the world around you squeeze you into its own mould" (Phillips). Isn't that just another way of

saying, "You are made for the skies, so don't let the world cram you into a cage"?

2. I think of Søren Kierkegaard, the respected Danish theologian, and his story of the wild duck flying south for winter. The duck saw an abundant supply of corn in a barnyard, swooped down, took a closer look, and decided to stop and spend the winter there eating corn. In the spring, when the other wild ducks flew back north, the wild duck tried to fly and join his friends, but he couldn't get off the ground. He was too fat, too tame, too domesticated. He remained trapped in the barnyard boredom, imprisoned by his greed and laziness. He was made for the skies but became crammed in a cage of his own making.

3. I think of Harry Emerson Fosdick, the famous pastor of Riverside Church in New York City, and his fascinating vulture story. It was a wintry day on the Niagara River below Buffalo, New York, when the vulture lighted on a carcass floating down the river and began to feed. He intended to feed until just before the falls and then break away and fly to safety. But as he and the carcass moved swiftly toward the falls, he tried to fly away but he couldn't— his claws had frozen on this cold wintry day to the carcass, and he plunged over the falls to his death. He made for the skies but crammed in a cage of his own doing. He meant to break free at the last moment, but his talons were frozen. He was imprisoned by the clutch of his claws.

There is a sermon there somewhere. Our hands freeze to that which we feed on and although we are meant for the skies, we get crammed in a cage.

If we are self-centered, we are crammed into the cage of selfishness.

If we feed on defeat, we are crammed into the cage of negativism.

If we are hooked on tranquilizers, alcohol, or drugs, we are crammed into the cage of escapism.

If we always maintain the status quo, we are crammed into the cage of the closed mind.

If we are jealous or resentful, we are crammed into the cage of hate.

If we constantly talk about others, we are crammed into the cage of gossip.

If we are anxiety-ridden, we are crammed into the cage of fear.

And if we are trapped in any of these cages, then we are headed for a fall. We have lost our freedom. We are made for the skies and crammed in a cage.

It's sad but true, isn't it? Many people do let one little thing—such as prejudice, envy, a bad temper, a worried spirit, nervous tension, or hostility—eclipse their lives and enslave them.

What about you? Is there any one thing that's making a slave of you? You were made for the skies, you were meant for greatness, but are you letting something imprison you? Are you letting stubborn pride, selfishness, prejudice, hate, jealousy, or apathy cram you in a cage?

It's something to think about, isn't it?

CHAPTER 31

I DISTINCTLY REMEMBER FORGETTING THAT!

PHILIPPIANS 3:12-14

A good memory is a wonderful gift! Most of us wish we could improve our memories. How terrific it would be, we think, to have an infallible memory, an instant recall of all former impressions.

The truth is that there aren't many photographic memories around. In fact, most of us suffer from memories that fail us at the most inopportune times. The saying goes, "The mind is a marvelous thing, but sometimes it is a freak. The only time it ever sits down is when I stand up to speak."

But as important as a good memory may be, the power to forget some things may be equally valuable. At first glance, most of us think that we need no help in the forgetting department. Our memories let us down at the most critical times.

We forget names, appointments, addresses, dates, and even words; the result is often embarrassing and frustrating. As troublesome as these circumstances are, it is still a good thing to learn to forget some things. With that in mind, consider these vignettes:

+ Two men are talking. First man: "My wife has a terrible memory, the worst memory I ever heard of." Second man: "Forgets everything, huh?" First man: "No! Remembers everything!"

+ Clara Barton, founder of the American Red Cross, was once reminded of a cruelty done her. Serenely she replied: "I distinctly remember forgetting that!"

+ A friend of mine said to me recently: "My father taught me that one of God's greatest blessings is the ability to forget some things and go on with life."

+ The great people have always known that there are some things you are better off forgetting. The apostle Paul knew this and made it clear in his letter to the Philippians when he said, "Forgetting what lies behind . . . I press on!" Paul had learned that as wonderful as it is to remember, it is also good sometimes to forget. It is good sometimes to intentionally remember to forget!

Let me illustrate this further by underscoring some specific things that we may want to remember to forget.

1. We may need to forget our past accomplishments. Past victories, if we dwell on them, can make us lazy, spoiled, or complacent. It's not healthy to live in the glow of past successes for too long. We must constantly press ahead, looking for new thresholds and new challenges.

2. We may need to forget our past hurts—past hurts that dampen our spirits, drain away our energies, and poison our souls. In other words: Don't nurse grievances! Don't give in to self-pity! Don't wallow in your heartaches! Put them behind you and go on with life.
3. We may need to forget our failures. Remember how the song "Pick Yourself Up" puts it? "Pick yourself up, dust yourself off, and start all over again." No failure need be final. We can start over, make a new beginning, try again.

Several years ago, a newspaper reporter interviewed one of the country's best-known psychologists and asked, "What do you try to do for those who come to you for treatment?" The psychologist answered, "Our objective is to free the patient from the tyranny of the past." How important that is. We all have past failures that haunt us, but we don't have to be defeated by them. No one is ever a failure so long as he can say, "I'd like to try again!"

The point of all this is that poor memory is not always bad. There are some things we need to purposefully forget.

++++++++++++++++++++++++++++++++++++++

CHAPTER 32

THE POWER OF LOVE

1 CORINTHIANS 13

Some years ago, I was teaching a course in religion at what was then Lambuth University in Jackson, Tennessee. I was trying to help the students understand creative ways to approach the Scriptures and to catch the excitement of the relevance of the Bible for our time and their lives.

To make this vivid for them, one morning I put the class in four groups—one group in each corner of the room. Each group was then given a section of the apostle Paul's "love chapter" (1 Corinthians 13) and asked to paraphrase it by putting it in their own words.

"Read it . . . understand it . . . and then re-state it in your own words," the students were told. When they finished, we combined their paraphrases and came out with a modern version of 1 Corinthians 13, which they entitled "Love Like Wow!"

Though I may be able to speak French, Spanish, and Japanese, and even rap with the angels, if I have not love, my speech is not more than a broken guitar or a scratched record.

I may preach like Billy Graham, have the brains of Einstein; I may have all the faith needed to put a Volkswagen into a phone booth; but if I have not love, I am nothing;

I may give the shirt off my back, and even smash my Steppenwolf albums (just to please my folks), but if I have not love, it does me no good;

Love is tolerant and tender;

Love is not stuck up or uptight;

Love is not facetious or snooty or touchy;

Love is not pessimistic;

Love does not dig in the gutter or hunt for gossip, but rather is happy with the truth;

Love never cops out. Its faith, hope, and patience never fail.

Love can outlast life (and the universe).

People will take forever, but never get things done. The Beatles may shake the world, but it is soon spent.

When perfect truth comes, life begins to take on meaning. And when love comes, the meaning of life is complete.

When I was a dumb kid, my whole life was wrapped in selfishness and egotism, but now I have grown up and matured some and I am embarrassed by, and ashamed of, vain self-centeredness.

Looking at life now is like looking in those crazy mirrors at the carnival. Things are twisted, distorted, fuzzy, but someday God will really open our eyes and then we will be able to see life as God intended it.

Meanwhile, our survival kit must be supplied with faith, hope and love.

Love is the greatest—so put love first!

Paul was right on target in his "love chapter," and those students were pretty much on target in their contemporary paraphrase. Both underscored the secret of life . . . and the word is "love!"

Love is indeed the key to meaningful living. It is indeed the single most important thing in the world. If we miss that—if we miss love—then we have missed life.

Love is the one thing that is always right, always on target. If we fail in our loving, then we fail altogether.

You see, you may have an educated mind, you may give your talents to worthwhile causes, you may rise to places of prominence in the eyes of other people, you may live an honorable and decent life.

But even after you have done all those things, if you have left love out of your life, you have missed it—you have missed the whole point of life.

The absence of love is the reason many people today feel unhappy and restless. They feel empty and unfulfilled because they have not learned how to love.

Love is the one quality about which we can say, "If a person has this, his life is good." Without this, no matter what else we may have or do, our life is a failure. If we fail in our loving, we fail altogether.

So, as those college students told it: "Put love first."

◆◆◆

CHAPTER 33

THE DANGERS OF SUCCESS

MATTHEW 5:6

As strange as it may sound, our own successes can ruin us, if we are not careful. Our own successes can make us lazy or spoiled or complacent or afraid to take new steps, to try new things, to risk new challenges, to think new thoughts.

Wasn't this the rich young ruler's problem? His "success" made him unable to respond to Jesus' call. His "success" made him afraid to try something new. His "success" caused him to turn away sorrowfully.

Remember that ancient legend about Moses' flute? It was the flute Moses played as he tended his flocks on the plains of Midian. Just before his death, Moses gave the flute to the priests, who would play it in worship services on high occasions. It was a simple inexpensive shepherd's flute, but it had a beautiful tone. Over the years, it was decided that Moses' flute should be more beautiful and ornate. So they covered it with gold and inlaid jewels. When they finished decorating the flute, it was beautiful. But there was only one thing wrong: the instrument would not play a note! It was beautiful, but it could not make a sound. It looked great, but it would not work anymore!

There is a crucial message for us here, namely this: our past successes can immobilize us if we dwell on them too much. I don't know a lot about boxing, but I know enough to understand two phrases that fight analysts use, phrases that carry over into other dimensions of life. I recently heard a former boxer talking on TV about an upcoming fight and he used these two phrases. He predicted that one fighter, who had been very successful as a boxer, would lose because he had become a "fat cat." And he predicted that the other boxer would win because he was a "hungry fighter"!

Although I am not a boxing expert, I knew what he was saying. "Fat cats" are those in any field who, because of their past successes, have become spoiled, lazy, complacent, self-satisfied, pompous, and prideful. Whereas the "hungry" are those who strive, struggle, work, dream, reach, sacrifice, and are willing to pay the price to get better.

As I thought of this, somehow my mind darted to the words of Jesus. "Blessed are those who hunger and thirst for righteousness." And the words of Paul: "Forgetting what lies behind . . . I press on!"

Sadly, the truth is that many lives have been shriveled by success. On the one hand, when we fail at something, we feel challenged to rise up and try again, to prove our worth, and to show the world that we can do this. On the other hand, after our successes, we can be so easily tempted to relax and give in to a lazy complacency.

There are so many places where the truth of this thought is evident. There is the athlete who does well and then relaxes on his press clippings and loses the sharpness that originally made him great. Or the writer who could be masterful, but settles for mediocrity; or the politician who starts out to serve the people and then after early success wants the people to serve him; or the artist who achieves greatness but then, caught in his successful self-importance, loses his touch. Or how about the graduate who finishes at the top of his class but never measures up to his potential because he dwells on what he has done, rather than what remains to be done?

Have you considered, too, how easily this can happen in our spiritual lives? So many of us look back on the place, date, and time when we felt some moving experience with God, and this is fine, but we must not be content to park by that experience.

We must *press on!*

Somehow, we must move on to greater depths of faith and commitment. And that only comes through struggle, discipline, and perseverance. We are always tempted to stop, to quit, to rest on our laurels, but people of faith never stop. They keep on keeping on! They keep on hungering and thirsting after righteousness.

◆◆

CHAPTER 34

CHANGE YOUR ATTITUDES AND CHANGE YOUR LIFE

PSALM 19:7-14

Her name was Madeleine. She was one of the outstanding book reviewers in the nation, and an inspiration to many, not only because of her brilliant talent as a book reviewer but also because of her inner strength, her determination, and her great attitude that helped her overcome a terrific hurdle called polio.

Listen to her words:

> When I was three years old, I was one of the first nine people to have the disease diagnosed as poliomyelitis in New York State; and I was nearly sixteen before a series of long hospital stays and endless operations enabled me to put my feet on the floor and with the aid of heavy braces and crutches to begin to walk.
>
> I've never been able to walk across an open field or play a game of tennis or go to a dance. I know the meaning of frustration.
>
> I've had to work hard on my attitudes. I couldn't permit myself to be eaten out by the virus of self-pity or jealousy for those who possessed something without any effort that I have worked my head off to gain and will never have.

> The Christian answer is to move forward. If life gives us a
> lemon, then we must make it into a refreshing lemonade.

And that's just what she did, and she did it with a great Christian attitude. Attitude is so important in life. We can't emphasize that too much! The great Coach Vince Lombardi once said, in effect, that football is 75 percent attitude.

The writer of Proverbs said that as a man thinks in his heart, so is he. The meaning is that whatever gets hold of you in your innermost being is the thing that controls your life. Whatever we really think about, dwell upon, give ourselves to, that is what controls our lives.

Jesus realized this when he said to seek first the kingdom of God and everything else will be cared for. The apostle Paul expressed it by saying: "I appeal to you, brethren—to present your bodies as a living sacrifice, holy and pleasing to God" (Romans 12:1, paraphrased). In other words, to give everything, even your attitudes, completely to God. The psalmist put it powerfully like this: "Let the words of my mouth and the meditation of my heart be acceptable to you, O LORD, my rock and my redeemer" (Psalm 19:14).

Life is determined by attitude. You change your attitudes and you change your life. One of the most fascinating books I have read that underscores this is Viktor Frankl's *Man's Search for Meaning*. Dr. Frankl, an Austrian psychiatrist, was a prisoner of war in Nazi concentration camps. During his imprisonment he noticed that some prisoners who looked physically strong and robust were actually weak because of their attitudes, and that others, because of their positive attitudes, were strong and an inspiration to all in the camp. In his book, Dr. Frankl has this marvelous paragraph. Read closely:

> We who lived in concentration camps can remember the men who walked through the huts comforting others, giving away their last piece of bread. They may have been few in number, but they offer sufficient proof that everything can be taken from a man but one thing: the last of the human freedoms—to choose one's attitude in any given set of circumstances, to choose one's way.

The apostle Paul said, "Don't let the world around you squeeze you into its own mold" (Phillips). The world around us doesn't have to determine what we are. Circumstances do not make us. Our attitudes determine who we are and what kind of world we really live in. Captain Eddie Rickenbacker once wrote: "If you think about disaster you will get it. Brood about death and you will hasten your demise. Think positively and masterfully, with confidence and faith, and life becomes more secure, more fraught with action, richer in achievement and experience."

With God's help and by his amazing grace, you can change your attitudes and change your life! You see, your destiny is not a matter of chance. It is a matter of choice. Every person chooses his own destiny by his or her attitudes toward life.

CHAPTER 35

THE BEAUTY OF UNIQUENESS—OR IT'S OK TO BE DIFFERENT

ROMANS 12:3-13

A psychologist in Houston, Texas, Roger Birkman, developed a personality profile a number of years ago that suggests that, broadly speaking, there are four different personality styles.

First, there is the autocratic doer—the action-oriented or strong-willed person who "means business" and gets things done sometimes by taking charge and telling others exactly what to do.

Second, there is the detailed planner who "plans the work and then works the plan!" This personality is precisely what the name implies: one who thinks things through in great detail and wants things done neatly and in order—and very systematically.

The third personality style is the enthusiastic salesman, a person who feels things strongly, is gregarious, outgoing, and emotionally charged. This person comes on strong and wants others to plug in to the feeling level. The enthusiastic salesman is a "people person" and wants others to experience what he or she is feeling and wants to "sell others" on his or her way of doing things and getting things done.

A fourth personality style is the artistic poetic philosopher, a person more "soulful," more tuned in to beauty, reverence, awe. This personality is creative—one who enjoys quiet and pensive moments of solitude, one who can "tune in" to the wonders of the universe and the mysteries of life.

Dr. Birkman had an interesting way of clarifying these four personality styles, so we can recognize them more quickly and easily:

> Imagine that you have nine cats in a house and your task is to get the cats out of the house. How would you do it?
>
> The autocratic doer would take matters into his own hands. He would say, "Scat," and the cats had better get out if they know what's good for them. He means business and he is going to get this job done.
>
> The detailed planner, on the other hand, numbers the cats one, two, three, four, five, six, seven, eight, and nine with nine neat tags attached neatly to the collars of each of the cats in calligraphy and then the detailed planner puts nine neat holes in the wall and numbers them one through nine. Cat one must go out hole one, cat two must go out hole two; cat three must go out hole three, and if cat four runs out through hole seven, the detailed planner is completely frustrated! For him it must be thought out systematically and worked out neatly. You plan the work and work the plan!
>
> The enthusiastic salesperson would say, "You want me to get cats out of a house? Piece of cake! No problem!" And then the enthusiastic salesperson would get some warm milk and cat food, go out in the front yard, call, "Here kitty, kitty," and convince the cats that they're a lot better off outside anyway.
>
> The artistic poetic philosopher, meanwhile, says, "What in the world am I doing worrying about cats?"

Now, there are some important insights to grab hold of here out of Birkman's personality profile. For one thing, it makes clear that we are different! We are unique and differentness is here to stay!

We are different—different in appearance, in approach, in ideas, in tone, in emphasis. Some are action-oriented; some are pensive and thoughtful; some are loud; some are quiet; some are poetic; some are autocratic. Some plan, some sell, some think, and some do!

We are different! We have different personalities, temperaments, skills, priorities, gifts, attitudes, opinions, and styles. And it's OK to be different! As a matter of fact, God must love differentness and variety because he made so much of both.

The Scriptures speak of differentness as a necessary blessing. Some are "apostles, some prophets, some evangelists, some pastors and teachers," says the apostle Paul. "The body does not consist of one member but of many" and all are needed, all are helpful.

We are different and it's all right to be different, as long as we are loving, kind, tolerant, respectful, and understanding about it.

But here is the rub. If we are insecure, then people different from us threaten us, and we can become scared and panicky and we react by trying to force our way on them.

We want to make them be like us. We want to make them do it our way. We feel compelled to prove that my way is the right way, the valid way, the only way. And we may think the other person is cruel or stupid or insensitive.

But don't you see how wrong this is? God is so big that there are many different pathways to him. Our religion is the response of our unique personality to the personality of God. And since our individual personalities are different, our individual pathways to God are different.

Every person is a unique child of God. We must not miss that. We dare not take that uniqueness away!

CHAPTER 36

FRIENDSHIP WITH GOD

JOHN 15:12-17

It is said Elizabeth Barrett Browning once asked fellow writer Charles Kingsley: "What, sir, is the secret of your life? Tell me, that I may make mine beautiful too."

"Madam," Kingsley answered, "I had a friend."

With that answer, Charles Kingsley put his finger on a highly significant insight in Christian theology: God is on our side. God is not the enemy, not the adversary. God is not hostile or vengeful or impersonal. Rather, God is our friend!

Now, if God is our friend, then religion may be defined as "friendship with God." With this in mind, it is interesting to note that the things that enable human friendships to be built and to survive are the same things that keep our friendship with God fresh, vibrant, and alive.

Great friendships do not just happen. They have to be built. They have to be cultivated, nurtured, and preserved. If we can discover how human friendships are set up and kept going and then put those same principles to work in our friendship with God, then we can expect significant results.

With that as a backdrop, consider the four basic elements of friendship, the things that enable friendships to survive, and notice how closely related they are to our relationship with God, or better put—our friendship with God.

1. FRIENDSHIPS SURVIVE BY ASSOCIATION. That is, the friends most real to us are those with whom we associate most. The friends most real to us are those with whom we spend time.

There is an old saying, "Absence makes the heart grow fonder," and I'm sure there is some truth in that. But there may be more truth in that other saying, "Out of sight, out of mind." The spiritual application of this principle is obvious.

If we want our friendship with God to be alive and vibrant, then we must associate with him, stay close to him, spend time with him, keep in touch with him.

2. FRIENDSHIPS SURVIVE BY EXPRESSION. That is, friendship grows as we express it. Friendship is strengthened as we tell each other of our love. We are so made that no thought, no feeling, no impulse is fully ours until we have expressed it. Express your love in words and deeds, and the love becomes more real, more solid. This is true, too, in our friendship with God.

Isn't this what the church is about? As we worship God, as we pray to him, as we sing our hymns, as we say our creeds, as we study and discuss in Sunday school, as we serve God in word and deed, our friendship with God is strengthened.

3. FRIENDSHIPS SURVIVE BY DEVOTION. That is, friendship is kept alive and fresh by commitment and trust.

Once a woman wrote to an advice columnist: "Three times I married for love and all three ended in divorce. Is it all right if I marry this fourth time for money? (Signed) Not Sure." The columnist answered, "Dear Not Sure: You don't know what love is. Love is the giving of oneself in complete devotion to another!" Friendship that is real is rooted in complete commitment and nowhere is this truer than in our friendship with God.

4. FRIENDSHIPS SURVIVE BY AFFECTION. That is, a hug, a handshake, a kiss, a touch—these things build friendship. But, how do we hug God? Well, the answer is: by hugging his children, by reaching out and touching his children.

If we want a good friendship with God that is alive and fresh and growing, then the way to achieve it is to spend time with God, to express our love for him in word and deed, to give ourselves in complete devotion to God and the church, and to touch God with affection by touching his children.

CHAPTER 37

OUR FATHER

MATTHEW 6:7-13

Some years ago, when I was in seminary, I had a classmate from Detroit, Michigan, named Paul Hawks, who had a fascinating life story and a dramatic life experience that led him into the ministry.

He was a U.S. soldier in Korea during the Korean conflict. One night Paul got lost on a scouting patrol. Inadvertently, he wandered into enemy territory and for several days he hid out in the wilderness like a frightened animal trying to survive and get back to safety.

But eventually, he was captured and was made a prisoner of war. The stark details of what he experienced are much too horrifying to recount. It is sufficient to say that he was subjected to all kinds of physical and emotional abuses and indignities.

For example, on two occasions he was compelled by the enemy guards to dig his own grave and then stand in front of it as a firing squad marched out, raised its rifles, and squeezed the triggers. But nothing happened! The rifles did not fire. The hammers fell on empty guns. It was a form of mental torture.

Later, amidst the cold Korean winter, they poured ice-cold water on Paul Hawks's head—over and over—bucket after bucket, until he became the victim of complete amnesia.

He could not remember anything. It sounds strange to say, but the only thing he could remember was that he could not remember! He knew there was something in his past, but he could not remember anything. It was a "dark night of the soul" for Hawks! He didn't know who he was, where he had come from, or what he was doing there. He didn't know even his name.

Hawks sat in that prison camp in Korea day after day, night after night, trying desperately to remember something, trying to pull something out of his suddenly darkened past. Weeks passed with no results. Then one evening, something broke through.

Finally, he remembered something from his past. He remembered two words: "Our Father." That's all; just those two words. He began to work with that phrase. Hour upon hour, day after day, he repeated those two words, trying to pull something else out of his lost memory.

Then something else came: "Who art in heaven . . . Our Father, who art in heaven . . ." Hawks repeated that over and over until he remembered "hallowed be thy name." He went on like that, until he had reconstructed the entire Lord's Prayer.

Then he remembered his parents, who had taught him the prayer. He remembered his home, his church, his neighborhood, his country—and his name.

Hawks rebuilt his memory, reconstructed his life, and rediscovered his name around the Lord's Prayer and more specifically around those opening two words. Isn't that incredible?

So much can be learned from it. Let me quickly underscore three observations about it.

First, I don't want any of us to have to go through what Hawks went through. No one should. But wouldn't it be something if each of us could rediscover ourselves and reconstruct our lives around those two words: "Our Father"? Not "My Father," but "Our Father." If everyone saw every other person as a child of God, as a person of integrity and worth, as a brother or sister who shares the same heavenly Father, it would change the world!

Second, through that dark experience, Paul Hawks not only rediscovered his name, but God gave him a new name; no longer was he Paul Hawks, prisoner of war, he was now Paul Hawks, minister of God. He was called to preach through that dark night experience.

A third observation is that this story portrays in a highly dramatic way a common experience that psychologists and theologians call an identity crisis. Few will ever have amnesia, but on another level, each of us has to ask, "Who am I?" "What is my name?"

It is also a fact that sometimes we have to go through a traumatic experience—a dark night of the soul—before we are jolted into seeing ourselves as we really are and knowing what our real name is.

The spiritual question every person must ask is "Who am I really?" or "What really is my name?" The first two words of the Lord's Prayer help us answer that. When we say "Our Father" and mean it, we are saying who we are: the beloved children of God! When we live under the "Our Father" concept, it sets us free to love God and to love all other people.

CHAPTER 38

THE PARABLE OF THE LOCKSMITH

MATTHEW 28:16-20

R emember with me the parable of the locksmith.

Once there were some slaves in prison. The slaves had been in prison so long that they had forgotten they were slaves and that they were in prison.

In fact, they decided that they were free and that the walls surrounding them did not imprison them at all, but rather imprisoned the people outside because they often could hear cries of pain from the other side of the wall.

Once some of them escaped, but they came back. They told of wandering in the wilderness for years, of having to fight for their homes, of the problems of government, the cruelty of war, and of never-ending problems and anxieties out there in the world.

So they came back to the prison, back to the calm, secure, unchanging, less risky prison.

"Life is easier in this prison," they said to themselves, and "Since prison is supposed to make life harder, then we must not be in prison."

"Those people outside are the slaves," they said over and over and over again. "They are the prisoners, not us," they cried and went right on believing that they were free.

Of course, their existence was not always peaceful and quiet. Once a young locksmith came in over the wall. He not only told them that they were slaves and in prison, he did something even more drastic—he broke the locks on the prison door!

With the door unlocked and open, the cries of pain and need from the other side of the wall were no longer muffled, but rang louder and louder!

Then the young locksmith had the audacity to tell the inmates that now they were free, and what's worse, that they ought to live *outside* the prison. He told them to go out into the world, to take love and caring and healing to the needy world.

A few of the prisoners believed him, but most of them said he was crazy. Anyone could see that true happiness and peace were where they were. Then they decided that this young locksmith was a social menace and that for the good of the community, he ought to be done away with before he ruined things. He had to be silenced, they said, because he was upsetting the people with these strange ideas.

So they accused him of being a troublemaker and had a quick trial. He was declared guilty and executed for the good of the community.

His followers were afraid, confused, and quiet during the trial and execution. But when they discovered that the truth he had brought would not die, they took up his message. When they realized that there was no way the doors could be locked again, they took up his dream.

Many of them also were killed as troublemakers, but their companions kept preaching and teaching. And every once in a while, someone heard the message and believed. He accepted the fact of his slavery and his imprisonment and he went out the unlocked door to freedom in the world of pain, need, and service.

But many of the slaves kept on thinking that they were free. They never looked out the door for fear they might see someone in need or someone in trouble or some problem that needed solving. They put cotton in their ears to muffle the noise of cries for help.

They continued to believe that it was the people on the other side of the wall who were imprisoned. They just couldn't understand why the young locksmith had broken the locks on the prison door!

Now this is a striking parable. It's an unusual but relevant one for us because all about us, people are still imprisoned. People are still slaves to selfishness and pride and fear and anxiety. People are still imprisoned by hatred and prejudice. People are still bound by complacency and closed minds. People still misunderstand the meaning of freedom and salvation and deliverance.

But the good news of the parable is that Jesus Christ is the young locksmith. He breaks the locks and throws open the doors! He shows us that being human means being humane! He sends us out into all the world as servant people! He saves us not just *from* something but *for* something! He calls us to be the conscience of society!

He sends us out into the world of need and pain that we might be healers and peacemakers, that we might be the instruments of his love and mercy and compassion. He gives his life for us, that we might give our lives for others.

Christ breaks the locks on the prison door, so that we can go out and serve our neighbors in need, be the light of the world and the leaven in the loaf, and share God's love with a troubled world.

Saint Francis of Assisi sums it all up for us in his magnificent prayer. Listen closely:

> Lord, make me an instrument of Thy peace;
> where there is hatred, let me sow love;
> where there is injury, pardon;
> where there is doubt, faith;
> where there is despair, hope;
> where there is darkness, light;
> where there is sadness, joy.
> O Divine Master, grant that I may not so much seek
> to be consoled, as to console;
> to be understood, as to understand;
> to be loved, as to love;
> for it is in giving that we receive,
> It is in pardoning that we are pardoned,
> It is in dying that we are born to eternal life.

+++++++++++++++++++++++++++++++++++++++

CHAPTER 39

THERE ARE NO RESPECTABLE EXCUSES FOR NOT LOVING

JOHN 5:1-18

The Broadway play *The Elephant Man* has been acclaimed as one of the great plays of our time. During its opening season, it won all the major drama awards, including three Tonys, three Obies, the Drama Desk Award, and the New York Drama Critics Circle Award. It was made into a major motion picture.

The play, written by Bernard Pomerance, is based on the life of John Merrick, who lived in London during the latter part of the nineteenth century. Merrick was a horribly deformed young man whose physical appearance was so grotesque and whose head was so enormous that he was exploited as a freak called the Elephant Man in traveling sideshows.

Early in the play, he is abandoned by his manager. He is found scared, lonely, and helpless by a famous young doctor named Frederick Treves, who saves him from an angry mob, gives him a home in a prestigious London hospital, treats him, educates him, and introduces him to London society.

John Merrick—the Elephant Man—changes from a pathetic object of pity to the urbane and witty favorite of the aristocracy.

Watching the play, I was intrigued and deeply moved by that poignant scene in the basement of the Liverpool Street train station. Merrick feels frightened, confused, forsaken, abandoned, pushed out into a cruel world. A mob scene is occurring outside.

The angry crowd, threatened by his appearance, wants to rip him to pieces. The train conductor and a policeman have him holed up in the basement with the door barred, holding back the mob. They don't know what to do with Merrick. They think he is an imbecile and they treat him like one.

Interestingly, in that scene, as he pathetically cries out for help, he says the name "Jesus" four times. They can't understand what he is saying. Then when Dr. Treves arrives, the Elephant Man is finally able to communicate something that anyone could understand.

Gurgling up from deep within his soul came a pitiful, guttural, heart-wrenching cry—just two words: "Help me!"

As I experienced that touching moment in the play, my mind darted back to a similar experience in the fifth chapter of John's Gospel when Jesus comes to Bethzatha pool and heals the man who has been crippled and waiting for someone to help him for thirty-eight years. For thirty-eight years, he has been crying out (similar to the Elephant Man), "Help me!" For thirty-eight years, he has waited, but no one has helped him.

Why? Thinking about this recently, I began to try to imagine some of the "respectable excuses" the people back then might have devised to rationalize their failure to help this man who had been so needy for so long. Maybe they are the same respectable excuses we use ourselves today for failing to love.

RESPECTABLE EXCUSE ONE: Sometimes we don't love because we get accustomed to a bad situation. The man had no one to help him. Why? Because they didn't see him anymore.

He had become part of the landscape, part of the furniture. He had become so much a part of that scene that everybody took him for granted. They had long ago ceased to think his situation could be changed. He was as much a part of the territory as the five porches or the sheep gate.

This can happen to us. We can see something so much, become so accustomed to it, that we don't see it at all anymore—and thus we do nothing! So this excuse is not so respectable after all, is it?

RESPECTABLE EXCUSE TWO: Sometimes we fail to love because we say: "It's none of my business." Some people at the Bethzatha pool in Jerusalem may have seen the crippled man, but rationalized their inaction by saying, "It's none of my business. I never stick my nose into other people's affairs. I don't believe in interfering in other people's lives. Anyway, maybe he doesn't want my help."

Well, if helping other people is interfering, then Jesus was The Great Interferer. He walks to Bethzatha pool, sees this pitiful situation, and refuses to excuse himself. He makes it his business and helps the man, because his business was loving and caring. That's our business, too, so this excuse is really not so respectable.

RESPECTABLE EXCUSE THREE: Sometimes we excuse ourselves from loving people by saying, "I don't want to get involved!" In a 1964 murder so well known that a syndrome has been named after the victim, a twenty-eight-year-old woman named Kitty Genovese was attacked, beaten, and stabbed by a stranger in a respectable New York residential area. Later, police found a number of people (what was initially reported to be thirty-eight) had been aware of the attack. Questioned after the murder, almost every one of the witnesses gave the same "respectable" excuse: "I just didn't want to get involved."

RESPECTABLE EXCUSE FOUR: Sometimes we fail to love because we say, "What can one person do?" Don't you imagine that many people who saw the lame man at Bethzatha pool may have said: "Sure I see him there and I feel really sorry for him, but what can I do? What can one person do?"

The answer to that is simple—a whole lot! One committed person can do incredible things. One person consumed with love can turn the world upside down.

Well, the message is clear and obvious: there are no respectable excuses for not loving. We must not miss this. If we fail in our loving, we fail altogether!

✦✦✦✦✦✦✦✦✦✦✦✦✦✦✦✦✦✦✦✦✦✦✦✦✦✦✦✦✦✦✦✦✦✦✦✦

CHAPTER 40

JESUS, THE MESSAGE AND THE MESSENGER

MATTHEW 7:24-28

Dietrich Bonhoeffer put it well when he said of Jesus: "In him, the message and the messenger became one!"

When we look at the Sermon on the Mount, we see in a unique way the mind of Jesus. When we read it, we can't help remembering that he not only taught it, he lived it! He was the message and the messenger rolled into one.

He was a peacemaker, he was humble-minded, he was merciful and genuine, he was pure in heart. He refused to retaliate or resent or demand his rights. He was the "salt of the earth," a "light on a stand."

Now, in this message and in this messenger we see life as God meant it to be. Real life as God intended it! Sometimes I wonder with the songwriter "when will we ever learn?"

James Tucker Fisher was a pioneer in psychiatry. Dr. Fisher studied under Freud and for more than fifty years specialized in the study of psychosomatic medicine. At the close of his book A

Few Buttons Missing, he makes a powerful summary about a fascinating discovery he made:

> I dreamed of writing a handbook that would give a new and enlightened recipe for living a sane and meaningful life—a handbook that would be simple, practical, easy to understand and easy to follow. It would tell people how to live . . . what thoughts and attitudes and philosophies to cultivate and what pitfalls to avoid, in seeking mental health.
>
> I attended every symposium possible, took notes on the wise words of teachers and my colleagues who were leaders in the field. . . . And then quite by accident, I discovered that such a work had already been completed—namely, the Sermon on the Mount.
>
> I now believe this to be true: If you were to take the sum total of all the authoritative articles ever written by the most qualified of psychologists and psychiatrists on the subject of mental hygiene . . . if you were to combine them and refine them and cleave out all the excess verbiage . . . you would have an awkward and incomplete summation of the Sermon of the Mount. And it would suffer immeasurably through comparison.

The point is that for nearly two thousand years, we have held in our hands the key to life, the answer to the world's restless yearnings. Our problem is that we are not so sure we can trust it.

"Did Jesus really mean it?" we ask. This business of "being meek, turning the other cheek, responding to evil with goodness, loving the enemy, going the second mile . . . Did Jesus really mean that?" we wonder.

Some years ago, there was a young professional baseball player who prided himself in being a great hitter. He knew that he could make it big in the major leagues if he could just get his chance, because he was confident of his ability as a batter.

For several years, he bounced around in the minor leagues. Then one year toward the end of the season, the major league parent team brought him up to help it as it was in the thick of a heated pennant race.

This was his chance. He was on a major league team—a rookie, but nevertheless, a member of a prestigious major league baseball team.

Promptly, they put him on the bench! Day after day went by and the rookie was itching to bat. He wanted to show them what he could do. He wanted to show the world that he was a great hitter.

Finally, one day the manager called for the rookie to pinch-hit. This was the dramatic moment he had dreamed of for so long: a crucial game, last inning, score tied, a runner on first base. This was his big moment.

The rookie's heart pounded with excitement as he stepped into the batter's box. Routinely, he glanced down toward the third-base coach. He couldn't believe his eyes! They were giving him the signal to "sacrifice."

"To sacrifice" means to bunt, to make an out on purpose to advance the runner to second base in the hope that the next hitter can bring him in. "To sacrifice" means to give your "life" at bat for the good of the team.

The rookie ignored the signal, took three hefty swings, and struck out. When he returned to the dugout, he was met by a red-faced irate manager, who said, "Son, what's the matter with you? Didn't you see the signal to sacrifice?"

"Yes, sir, I saw it," said the rookie. "But, I didn't think you meant it!"

"I saw it, but I didn't think you meant it!" Isn't that what we say to God? On page after page of the Scriptures, God says to us, "Sacrifice! Sacrifice! Love others! Lay down your life for others! Sacrifice yourself for the good of the team! Lose yourself! Be self-giving!"

That's what God says to us. That is God's signal to us, but we are not so sure he means it. Well, Jesus showed us that he means it—on a cross!

◆◆◆◆◆◆◆◆◆◆◆◆◆◆◆◆◆◆◆◆◆◆◆◆◆◆◆◆◆◆◆◆◆◆◆◆

CHAPTER 41

WHO'S IN CONTROL?

MARK 1:14-20

It was late on a Tuesday afternoon. The middle-aged man sitting across from me was frustrated. He was talking nonstop, emotionally venting his aggravation. Suddenly, he came right to the point: "It's Mother. She runs my life completely. All I ever do is try to please her. What Mother wants, Mother gets. I'm just not in charge of my life!"

His last comment raises an interesting set of questions. Who is really in charge of your life? Who is really in control? Are you? Do you want to be?

The truth is that many people today are not in charge of their lives. They are not really in control. Rather, they are controlled by other influences or by past events or by chemical substances or by inner problems or by other people or by paralyzing fears.

Let me be more specific by citing some examples:

1. Some people are controlled by outer circumstances. They just flow with the circumstances. Like a thermometer, they just register the climate. They never initiate anything; they only react to the circumstances. If it's gray and dreary outside, they are gray

and dreary inside. The circumstances of life dictate what their spirit will be or what their attitudes will be. They are prisoners of their circumstances.

People who let outer circumstances take charge of their lives like to play the "if only" game: "If only I had another job." "If only I could get married." "If only I could get un-married." "If only my circumstances were different . . . I would be happy."

Of course, the "if only" game doesn't work. It only dupes us and makes us more miserable and causes us to fail to face reality. It keeps us from dealing with our circumstances creatively.

Remember the story of the two men who were talking one day when one said, "I guess I'm doing fine under the circumstances." The other man responded: "What do you mean 'under the circumstances'? What are you doing under them? Get on top of them!" Precisely, but some people never learn to do that and they let circumstances take charge of their lives.

2. Then some people are controlled by other people, by some dominating person in their lives, or by peer pressure. I guess all of us to some degree want the sanction and approval of others, and we are probably affected by other people more than we realize.

But, it must be said that approval of our peers is NOT the ultimate concern of people of faith for at least a couple of reasons.

For one thing, we can't always go along with the crowd because our calling is to be the "conscience of the crowd," the "conscience of society." Sometimes we must say no, not a pietistic or arrogant no, but a no that is firm and solid and rooted in our principles. Carl Sandburg once told of a circus lizard that changed colors to blend in with whatever circumstances he encountered.

Put him on a brown suit to blend in. Put him on a green shirt and he would turn green. All went well until one day someone put him on a plaid sport coat. The lizard had a nervous breakdown trying to blend in!

Then, too, the crowd can be fickle. We can't always follow the popular fad. We have to know who we are and what we believe and be controlled by that and not by the latest craze. Some people never find out who they are; they just follow the crowd and let other people control their lives.

3. Still others are controlled by overbearing emotions, such as resentment, anger, jealousy, envy, bigotry, hatred, or selfishness. These powerful emotions can take control of our lives and run our lives and destroy us like spiritual cancers.

4. There is another option, a better way: we can follow Jesus Christ! We can put our trust in him. We can give our unwavering allegiance to him. We can trust the promise of God to always be with us in every circumstance of life and be strengthened by his presence to be our true best selves. We can put him and the doing of his will first in our lives. When we do that, when we love God and people, everything else falls in place. Love for God and people—that is the controlling force for people of faith!

✦✦✦✦✦✦✦✦✦✦✦✦✦✦✦✦✦✦✦✦✦✦✦✦✦✦✦✦✦✦✦

CHAPTER 42

WHAT CAN ONE PERSON DO?

ISAIAH 6:1-8

Let me begin with a parable. Once there was an old doctor in a small French village who was about to retire. For many years, he had served the people of the area diligently. He had been on call day and night. The people could not afford to pay him much, but that had made no difference to this devoted doctor. He had served them and cared for them ably and faithfully with great tenderness.

As the day of his retirement approached, the people wanted to make a concrete expression of their affection and gratitude. So it was proposed that on a given day, since they had so little money to give, they each would bring a pitcher of wine from their cellars and pour it into a large barrel placed in the village square, which in turn would be presented to the doctor, as an expression of their love and appreciation. The day arrived and all day long the people were seen coming from far and near and pouring their offerings into the barrel.

Then when the evening came, the barrel of wine was taken to the doctor's humble residence and presented to him, with all the inevitable speeches by the village mayor and other community leaders.

When the presentation was over, the people applauded and said thank you, and then all the villagers went back to their homes and the old doctor was left alone with the memory of their warm love and affection. He went to the barrel and drew off a bit of the wine. Then he went into the house and sat in a comfortable chair before the fire and began to sip the wine. The first sip however was a shock. It tasted like water. He sipped again. It was water.

He went back to the barrel and drew off some more, thinking there must have been some strange mistake. But no, the barrel was filled with water.

He called the mayor and the mayor called the assemblymen and there were hurried consultations. Then, slowly but surely, the truth was revealed . . . everyone in the town had reasoned: "My little pitcher of wine won't be missed. I have so little for myself. The others will take care of it. The little water I substitute will not be noticed. It will make no difference." But it did!

This poignant story may well be a parable for life in our time. Sometimes the bigness of life and the complexities of living in the twenty-first century tend to make us feel that we don't count.

"What can I do?" we ask. "What can one person do? I'm just one individual. My opinions don't matter. My vote doesn't mean much. My little portion won't be missed," we say.

This helpless feeling that "I don't have much to give" is one of the characteristic problems of our contemporary life. Many people today are burdened and oppressed by a sense of their own personal insignificance.

But Scripture says to us over and over that we do count, we do matter, that our little portion is significant. What if Jesus had thrown up his hands and said, "What can one person do?" What if Moses had said, "The Pharaoh won't listen to me!" What if Paul and Abraham and Peter and Isaiah had said, "The odds are against us!" What if Mary and Elizabeth had cried, "We have nothing significant to contribute"? What if Luther or Wesley or Saint Francis or Mother Teresa had each reasoned, "My little portion will never be missed"?

What if the little boy with five loaves and two fish had thought, "Not much can be done with such a little"?

The point is that God can make our little much. We can count. We can matter. We can influence. We can change things for the better. With the help of God, we can make a difference!

✦✦✦✦✦✦✦✦✦✦✦✦✦✦✦✦✦✦✦✦✦✦✦✦✦✦✦✦✦

CHAPTER 43

IS YOUR FAITH TOO SMALL?

ISAIAH 28:17-20

In 1650 Oliver Cromwell sent his famous message to the General Assembly of the Church of Scotland. It said: "I beseech you . . . think it possible you may be mistaken!" Then he urged them to read the twenty-eighth chapter of Isaiah.

He wanted them to learn from it the feebleness and futility of "little religion" or "small faith." In this chapter, the prophet Isaiah uses a colorful illustration to drive home his point: "The bed is too short to stretch oneself on it, and the covering too narrow to wrap oneself in it" (Isaiah 17:20).

Out of this humorous figure of the "too short bed" and the "too narrow covers," Isaiah is raising some haunting questions for us, namely: Is our religion too little? Is our thinking too narrow? Does our faith work? Is our faith big enough? Or is it too small?

Anyone who has ever spent a restless night on a short uncomfortable bed, or anyone who has ever tried to make it through a freezing night with inadequate covers, knows what Isaiah is say-ing. We know that such conditions make us miserable, cold, uneasy, frustrated, tossing and turning and wishing morning would hurry up and come.

Isaiah said that people who have a faith that is too small are this way. They are cold, restless, and unsatisfied. This is what Isaiah saw in his people—"too small faith," elaborate ceremony without moral content, empty religion, shallow faith.

He knew that this kind of empty religion might serve those who "sunned themselves" in the warmth of momentary prosper-ity, but when the night fell and the cold, frigid, blustering, howl-ing winds of trouble struck their lives, it would be inadequate. It would be like trying to get through a long cold night with a too short bed and too narrow covers.

Now, Isaiah calls us to the test, suggesting that each of us needs to examine our faith to see if it is equal to the demands of life and big enough for the days of our lives.

Well, how about it? How is it with you? Is your faith big enough? Or, is your faith too small? Let's check by looking at some specific measuring sticks for faith.

1. YOUR FAITH IS TOO SMALL WHEN IT MAKES YOU SATISFIED WITH YOUR SPIRITUAL ATTAINMENT. Good religion keeps on growing. It is always open to new truths from God. When we become self-satisfied or lazy or complacent, then our faith is too small.

2. YOUR FAITH IS TOO SMALL WHEN IT MAKES YOU CRITICAL OF OTHERS. Something is wrong with your

religion if it makes you "holier than thou" or if it causes you to pass judgment on others or if it causes you to feel that every person who does not agree with your theology is wrong or lost. Actually, genuine faith works just the other way around. It makes you not more critical of others but rather more loving toward others.

3. YOUR FAITH IS TOO SMALL WHEN IT CHANGES YOU OUTWARDLY BUT NOT INWARDLY. We can do the right things for the wrong reasons. We can do something outwardly that looks good, but at the same time be seething inside. If our motivations and inner attitudes are not right, then our faith is too small.

4. YOUR FAITH IS TOO SMALL WHEN IT DOESN'T WORK IN PRACTICAL DAY-TO-DAY LIVING. Good faith works now. Genuine religion touches our lives, our attitudes, our values, our morality, our relationships now. It makes us better people now. It is not an insurance policy for another day but a lifestyle that enables us to celebrate the present.

Some years ago, a minister received a letter from a young mother in which she told of what happened as she moved into a new subdivision just outside New York City. She told him that they had tried everything they could think of to make their new community something more than a real estate development. They tried organized recreation, community picnics, and square dancing. They formed a women's club and held bridge parties and started a garden club.

They had a parents' organization and evening discussion groups. They tried everything. But she pointed out that it was not until the church came that they changed from a subdivision into a community and became real neighbors to one another.

Good religion works now. It gives you a sense of partnership with God and people.

And, there is nothing small about that.

✦✦✦✦✦✦✦✦✦✦✦✦✦✦✦✦✦✦✦✦✦✦✦✦✦✦✦✦✦✦

CHAPTER 44

TELL ME, PLEASE, HOW TO BE HAPPY

PSALM 42:1-5

Well, it happened again this week. A young woman came to the church with tears in her eyes, despondent, depressed, saddened, burdened, filled with despair. She poured out her heart, and then rather suddenly blurted out, "Jim, tell me, please, how to be happy."

I don't know if I had ever heard anybody just openly express it like that, but in a sense every burdened person who comes to the church for help is saying that—"Tell me, please, how to be happy."

This young woman characterizes the emotional state of many people: People who are hurt or crushed or perplexed, broken-hearted, disillusioned, suffering from depression.

Not too long ago, I was reading a magazine article written by a psychologist who said that depression is Public Enemy Number One. And there are some weeks when I believe that to be true. All of us experience periods of depression or unhappiness, and the psalmist has expressed it for us, "Why are you cast down, O my soul, and why are you disquieted within me?"

Unhappiness seems to be a universal thing, and it comes from many sources. Some people are unhappy with their careers. They had hoped for great things; they had dreamed of working themselves up from office boy to president of the corporation and then suddenly they realize that it will never happen, and their hearts are broken.

Some people are unhappy because they lack social acceptance. They dream of high social standing and they try all their lives to step up the social ladder only to find that they can only get so far and that they may not be accepted above that certain place, and they are brokenhearted and crushed.

Some people are unhappy because they feel that their friends have let them down. They have trusted in somebody like you or me and they have discovered that we have feet of clay and somehow they feel that we have failed them.

Some are unhappy with their marriages. They still remember the glow as they stood at the altar and took the marriage vows and made a covenant with one another, but then over the months and years they have drifted apart and now where once there was love there seems to be bitterness and where once there was affection there seems to be negligence and indifference.

Some people are made unhappy by their children—strange as that may seem. It must be quite a blow to hold a little baby in your arms and have high hopes for him or her only in later years to have those hopes dashed. It must be quite a jolt.

And some people are unhappy because they don't seem to have any meaning in their lives. They are bored with life—they have no sense of purpose.

But all of these are crying out to the church and to the Christian faith—"Tell me, please, how to be happy."

How do we deal with this unhappiness? Well, obviously some people handle it all wrong. To escape the despair of unhappiness, millions flee to a temporary solace in liquor or drugs or overwork or purposeless activity. These don't help—they merely compound the problem.

What then does the Christian faith say about this? The words of the pastor J. Wallace Hamilton are very helpful and powerful here. He said: "Happiness is basically a by-product. It comes by indirection. To pursue it, to pounce upon it, to go directly after it is the surest way to miss it."

1. HAPPINESS IS A BY-PRODUCT OF INNER STABIL-ITY. Inner stability, not outer security. How we misunder-stand this! Every year in our country we spend billions and billions of dollars in a frantic pursuit of happiness—on things to do, places to go, stuff to swallow. Mistakenly, we think happiness is "out there" somewhere and we miss the "inner spirit" which really produces the only lasting happiness.

2. HAPPINESS IS A BY-PRODUCT OF WHOLENESS. Health, wholeness, holiness: they all come from the same root word and they mean "getting it all together." When we are "fragmentized" or pulled in all sorts of directions or

mixed-up in our priorities or values, the consequence is unhappiness. Happiness comes from wholeness, from "getting it all together."

3. HAPPINESS IS A BY-PRODUCT OF USEFULNESS. It is the by-product of being in service to God and to other people. It's the by-product of forgetting about yourself and reaching our in love and concern to others. Ralph Waldo Emerson once said it like this: "Happiness is a perfume you cannot pour on others without getting a few drops on yourself."

4. HAPPINESS IS A BY-PRODUCT OF LIVING IN DAY-TIGHT COMPARTMENTS, LIVING ONE DAY AT A TIME. Many people stay unhappy because they worry constantly about the skeletons of the past or the challenges of the future so much that they can't enjoy or celebrate the present moment. Someone once said that there are two days in each week that we don't have to worry about: yesterday and tomorrow. We are called to live only one day at a time—to celebrate the present.

5. HAPPINESS IS A BY-PRODUCT OF FELLOWSHIP WITH GOD. The psalmist asks the question: "Why are you cast down, O my soul? Why are you disquieted within me?" Then he gives an answer to this question by saying: "Hope in God; for I shall again praise him, my help and my God." This is the real and lasting source of happiness—fellowship with God.

✦✦✦✦✦✦✦✦✦✦✦✦✦✦✦✦✦✦✦✦✦✦✦✦✦✦✦✦✦✦✦✦

CHAPTER 45

THE DANGERS
OF OVERREACTING

MATTHEW 13:24-30

Much of the misery in the world today is caused by hasty, explosive overreaction.

Friendships are destroyed, marriages are disrupted, churches are split, wars are started, lives are lost, hearts are broken—because of impulsive overreaction.

Let me illustrate this with a few life vignettes.

A lady in our church was driving alone down Pine Hills Road. As she came out of a curve heading toward the McCane Creek Bridge, she drove into a nightmare experience that only a great faith and tenacious determination enabled her to survive.

As she rounded the curve, her right front wheel struck a bad place in the road, forcing the car over onto the right shoulder and out of control. Frightened (as all of us would have been), she jerked the steering wheel hard back to the left, but too strongly.

She overcorrected and the car caromed back all the way across the road and off the left side where it sideswiped the end of the bridge, catapulted eighty feet through the air over the creek, and landed, front wheels on the opposite bank with the rest of the car submerged in the water.

With water in the car up to her shoulders, with a broken left arm, broken ribs, a fractured neck, facial cuts, and crushed legs she struggled to keep her head above water. She waited for what must have seemed like an eternity and she prayed with all her might.

An hour-and-a-half later, thank God, help came. She not only survived that terrible ordeal, but became an inspiration to all of us who know her. But, isn't that an interesting parable for life?

The point is that it is so easy when under pressure to over-correct, to overreact, and sometimes the real dangers are in the overreaction.

✦ ✦ ✦

Have you heard about the bow-legged man who prayed all night, "Lord, make my legs straight. Lord, make my legs straight!"

Over and over and over, all night long he prayed, "Lord, make my legs straight." And, when he got up the next morning, he was knock-kneed! There is a sermon there somewhere.

✦ ✦ ✦

Recently, I read about a Methodist Sunday school teacher who taught children in the third grade Sunday school class. In her class she had twin girls who seemed happy and never missed church.

The twins came from a poor family and their dresses were worn and out of style, but it didn't seem to bother them, for every Sunday they were in their places at the Methodist church.

The Sunday school teacher, concerned about the twins, took up some money and bought them some beautiful new Sunday dresses. The next Sunday, the twin girls were missing. The teacher called their home immediately to see if they were sick.

"Oh, no, they are not sick," explained the mother. "They just looked so nice this morning in their new dresses that I sent them to the Presbyterian church." I guess our "overcorrections" can come back to haunt us.

✦ ✦ ✦

Do you remember young Mary O'Conner, a devout Catholic who fell in love with John Jones, a staunch Baptist? They wanted to get married, but Mary's mother objected to the idea of her Catholic daughter marrying a Protestant. Mary was heartbroken, but her mother suggested a solution.

"Sell him on the Catholic Church," she said. "Tell him about our great church and sacred traditions; tell him about our long history and great beliefs; tell him about our dedicated martyrs and noble saints. Go to him, Mary, sell him, be persuasive, get him to become a Catholic and then you can marry him."

Mary dried her eyes and went to see John. A little later, Mary returned home and burst through the door sobbing.

"What's the matter?" her mother asked, "Couldn't you sell him?"

"Sell him!" Mary cried. "I over-sold him and now he wants to become a priest!"

Here we see it again: the dangers of overreaction.

✦ ✦ ✦

We all should know this point well. We have seen it a hundred times in old Western movies. A man, suspected of wrongdoing, is put in jail to await trial. The judge has to come over from Dodge City, a three-day journey.

But some of the townspeople can't wait. They want their town purged of evil right now, although the evidence against the man is not conclusive. They quickly condemn the man, organize a lynch-mob, and march to the jail with torches and a rope to string up the suspect.

The sheriff holds them off. He tells them they can't do this; they can't take the law in their own hands; they can't condemn this man to death without a fair trial, they have no real conclusive evidence on this man and no right to kill him.

He says: "Be patient! Trust the courts! Wait for the trial! Only the judge has the right to determine whether or not the suspect is guilty. Be patient! Justice will be served and righteousness will prevail."

Of course, you remember from those old Westerns that almost every time it turned out that the mob was wrong and the suspect was innocent and the townspeople were embarrassed by their hasty, explosive overreaction.

One of the parables of Jesus in Matthew's Gospel underscores the danger of overreaction. It's the parable traditionally called "the parable of the wheat and the tares" or "the parable of the weeds among the wheat."

In the parable, Jesus is calling for patience and warning us against hasty, emotional, impulsive, violent action. "Be patient! Trust God! Trust the test of time! The truth will come out."

So, don't overreact!

+++++++++++++++++++++++++++++++++++++++

CHAPTER 46

WHAT DOES IT MEAN TO BE A CHRISTIAN?

MARK 10:17-22

From the story of the rich young ruler in the Gospel of Mark, we can learn in a backdoor kind of way the key of characteristics of Christian discipleship and, more precisely, what it means to be Christian or "Christ-like."

Remember the story with me. Jesus is on his way to Jerusalem (and the cross) when the rich young ruler runs up and kneels before him. Notice this now: he runs up (a sign of enthusiasm); he kneels down (a sign of respect and reverence). Thus, we can assume here that this young man is not trying to trap Jesus with loaded questions (as others tried), but that he is really sincere when he asks: "Good Teacher, what must I do to inherit eternal life?"

Jesus answers, "You know the commandments. Do not kill; do not commit adultery; do not steal or defraud or bear false witness; honor your father and mother."

Then the young man responds: "All these I have kept from my youth."

Jesus then looks at him with love and says to him: "But you lack one thing: Go, sell what you have and give to the poor and you will have treasure in heaven; then come follow me." At this, the rich young ruler turns away and leaves sorrowfully, for he is a wealthy man.

Here in the rich young ruler's failure to respond and follow, we find some basic insights into what it means to be Christian. Let me list a few and you will think of others.

FIRST, A CHRISTIAN IS ONE WHO SEES GOD THROUGH THE EYES OF CHRIST. That's the key thing about Jesus. He shows us what God is like. He gives God a face, and that face is love. Someone put it like this: "Jesus was God's way of getting rid of a bad reputation." Jesus came to show us that God is not an angry and hostile deity, not an impersonal cosmic force, but a loving father, a God of love and compassion who cares for all of his children. We don't have to be afraid of God or of life and its problems or challenges, because the Father is with us to see us through them. The rich young ruler didn't understand this, and frightened, he turned away.

SECOND, A CHRISTIAN IS ONE WHO SEES VALUE THROUGH THE EYES OF CHRIST. In the rich young ruler incident, Christ gives us a new way of looking at things, a new way of measuring what is important.

Sometimes we stress the rich young ruler's lack of commitment so much that we miss one of the key insights of this story— namely, Christ's way of measuring what's valuable!

Notice this. Here is a man who is a success. He has it all—wealth, youth, power—and yet here is the point we must not miss. There is something lacking, an emptiness, a hunger. Jesus sees right to the heart of it. He is not fussing at wealth here. Rather, he is saying, "Following me is the greatest treasure in the world. It is wealth beyond counting." Here Jesus is talking about not just the cost of discipleship, but the riches of discipleship, and he is saying that discipleship is better than dollars. It's the most valuable thing in the world.

THIRD, A CHRISTIAN IS ONE WHO SEES OTHER PEOPLE THROUGH THE EYES OF CHRIST. The overriding keynote of Christ's life and ministry was his concern for others, his love for other people.

Did you notice how this love for others is underscored in the rich young ruler story? Not only does Christ tell the young man to care for the poor and needy but also when they talk about the commandments (did you catch this?), they mention only those which deal with our relationships with other people. What do you make of this? No mention of love for God here. Why? Well, simply because this is the way we express our love for God best—by loving other people! As a friend of mine put it, "When I first became a Christian, I was so excited that I wanted to hug God. Over the years, I have learned that the way you hug God is to hug his people!"

FOURTH, A CHRISTIAN IS ONE WHO SEES LIFE THROUGH THE EYES OF CHRIST. When we look at life through the eyes of Christ, two things stand out—urgency and self-giving. The rich young ruler missed that. Yet this is what

Jesus had in mind when he said, "The kingdom is at hand"; that is, "Now is the time to serve the King of kings!" In fact, we could well describe Christ's life as "urgent self-giving." He saw every moment as a unique and urgent opportunity to give himself for others.

That's what it means to be a Christian—serving God and giving ourselves for the cause of Christ in every moment; seeing every day, every occasion as a special and urgent opportunity to be a "little Christ," to continue his message, his work, his love . . . or in other words . . . to have "Christ-ed Eyes."

✦✦✦✦✦✦✦✦✦✦✦✦✦✦✦✦✦✦✦✦✦✦✦✦✦✦✦✦✦✦✦✦✦✦✦✦✦✦✦

CHAPTER 47

SNATCHING DEFEAT FROM THE JAWS OF VICTORY

MATTHEW 27:1-10

Some years ago when we were living in Shreveport, Louisiana, our family went to the Gold Dome one evening to see a Centenary College basketball game. The Centenary Gents took control of the game early, got a good lead, but then somehow lost concentration and eventually lost the game on a last-second shot.

As we drove home, we listened to the post-game interview on the car radio. I was interested in what the coach had to say. With some exasperation, he said: "We just couldn't stand success out there tonight. We got ahead and we got cocky. We got a good lead and then we just quit. We lost our intensity. We became lackadaisical and sloppy. We forgot who we were and what we were out there to do. Our early success ruined us and once again we did it—we snatched defeat from the jaws of victory!"

That's a good parable for life because "snatching defeat from the jaws of victory" is a common occurrence in life.

How often we make a good start, but then we wear down or give up—unable to finish what we started. We start out fresh, eager, excited, only to later stick in the mud or stall on a steep hill or quit altogether when the going gets rough. Let me show you what I mean.

The telephone rang loudly in a police station in New York City. The sergeant at the precinct desk handled the call with dispatch. He knew exactly what to do, because he had handled this kind of call many times before. It was now routine, almost commonplace. Another inebriated man was dead or dying in the street gutter in the Bowery.

Quickly, the police and the emergency squad were on the scene, sirens blaring, lights flashing. They did their best to revive him, but it was too late. He had breathed his last.

Some of the curious onlookers familiar with the people and the happenings in the Bowery recognized the dead man in the gutter. He was a well-known Bowery character who sold shoestrings and cigarette butts for drinks.

He was in his late forties, they discovered later, but he looked seventy because of the kind of life he had been leading. In a sense, he had unconsciously committed suicide, drowning himself in a relentless sea of alcoholic drinks.

Another Bowery drunk had died. What's so unusual about that? It's a common enough occurrence, you may say.

Many of you have been to New York City and you have taken the bus tours and you have seen firsthand the heartbreaking sights of the Bowery—men and women begging for drinks or lying unconscious on sidewalks and in gutters, sleeping in alleys and deserted storefronts with only rumpled newspapers for cover.

That's what the police found that day, another man who had literally drunk himself to death. But when they got to the city morgue with his body there was something unusual. They found not only his identification papers, but they also found in his pocket a Phi Beta Kappa key. Further investigation revealed that he had been brought up in a fine home and had graduated from Harvard University summa cum laude with a perfect 4.0 academic record.

What had happened? Wouldn't you like to know the rest of the story? I'm sorry, I don't know any more. But out of what we do know of the story, one thing is clear: although he died that day in the Bowery, although it was there he breathed his last, obviously he had quit life long before physical death. Somehow over the years he had snatched defeat from the jaws of victory.

This true story is a dramatic symbol of an important spiritual insight: as long as we live, we face two kinds of desires: the desire to shrink back and quit on life and the desire to move forward through struggle to a greater fulfillment of life.

Sadly, far too many people like the man in the Bowery, although less dramatically than he, give in to the desire to quit. They begin with starry eyes, great fervor, ready to conquer the world and live life to the full. But then come problems, difficulties, nuisances, burdens, troubles, disappointments, heartaches.

Suddenly they feel hoodwinked and deceived, and they are ready to throw in the towel and give up. Then life is no longer life. It's merely a series of escapes.

No longer do they really live. They vegetate, they endure, they exist, they get by, they make it through the day, but in essence they have quit on life. They have snatched defeat from the jaws of victory.

Don't let that happen to you. Don't shrink back or give up! Our calling as people of faith is to move forward and celebrate life.

✦✦✦✦✦✦✦✦✦✦✦✦✦✦✦✦✦✦✦✦✦✦✦✦✦✦✦✦✦✦✦✦✦✦✦✦

CHAPTER 48

WHAT ARE THE QUESTIONS?

LUKE 9:18-25

The *Houston Chronicle* ran a story about a test given to some music students in an unidentified junior high school. Here are some of their interesting answers.

✦ "Music sung by two people at the same time is called a duel."

✦ "I know what a sextet is . . . but I had rather not say!"

✦ "A xylophone is an instrument used mainly to illustrate the letter X."

✦ "Dirges are music written to be played at sad, sad occasions, such as funerals, weddings, and the like."

✦ "Refrain means 'don't do it!' A refrain in music is the part you better not try to sing."

✦ "A virtuoso is a musician with real high morals."

✦ "J. S. Bach died from 1750 to the present."

✦ "Handel was half German, half Italian, and half English . . . He was rather large!"

Now, we can tell from the results of this music test that right answers are important. But have you stopped to think that the right questions are important too?

How essential it is to get the right answers matched with the right questions! Nowhere is this truer than in the faith experience. Let me show you what I mean.

It is common to see bumper stickers, posters, lapel buttons, and highway signs displaying the words: "Christ is the Answer." Of course, as Christians we believe this to be true. We believe that Christ is the answer, that he is the highest revelation of what God is like, and what God wants us to be like.

Isn't that what the word "revelation" means—a disclosure, an unfolding, new light, new meaning, new understanding? But the words "Christ is the Answer" must be more than religious cliché or pious platitude.

The serious student or thinker comes back and asks, "What are the questions? If Christ is the answer, what are the questions?" We do need to look at that, don't we, because the only way any answer can be relevant and meaningful for us is for us to relate that answer to the proper question.

Let me illustrate that. Remember how math books sometimes have the answers printed in the back of the book? You can always get the right answer, but the answers by themselves mean nothing. They become significant and meaningful only when they are related to the specific problems given back in the lessons of the textbook. Only then does learning and growth occur. It isn't enough to just know the answer. You have to also know the question.

"Christ is the answer," but what are the questions? The noted psychologist Erik Erikson is helpful here. He lists some developmental questions that every person must ask and answer creatively before that person can become whole or mature.

Christ came to bring us wholeness, to make us "whole," the Scriptures tell us. So look with me quickly at how Christ brings light and meaning and answers to these five basic questions which every person must answer before he or she can have full, abundant life.

1. The question of IDENTITY: Who am I?
2. The question of INTIMACY: Who am I in relation to others?
3. The question of FAITH: Why am I here?
4. The question of LOYALTY: To whom and to what will I be true?
5. The question of VOCATION: What is my uniqueness or special calling?

These were the questions the prodigal son grappled with and they are the questions every person must ask and answer before he or she can have real life.

Christ helps us answer these questions and his answer is good news. He tells us that we are the beloved and valued children of God, that God claims us as his children and loves us like the gracious father in the prodigal son parable.

We are God's beloved children, related to all other people as brothers and sisters in his family. We are family, and we should live together in love and harmony and with respect and understanding. We are here to share this good news that God cares and he wants us to be caring.

We are here to love God and love people. We are here to serve God and trust him and be loyal to him even when times are hard. We are here to discover our own unique and special way to help continue the ministry of love which Christ began.

++++++++++++++++++++++++++++++++++++

CHAPTER 49

LIFE IS MUCH TOO SHORT FOR PETTINESS

LUKE 6:27-38

Pettiness is a spiritual cancer. To be *petty*, according to *Webster's Dictionary*, is to be "small in nature, trifling, mean or ungenerous."

How often pettiness cuts us off from God, from other people, and from the church!

I'm thinking of a man I know who is a fine singer. He has an excellent tenor voice, but he has not sung in church for more than twenty years. Some twenty-three years ago, he was active in his church's music program, sang in the choir, and was the church's main soloist.

But then he went to a convention in New York City and discovered that some of the large churches there pay their choir members. So, when he returned home, he gave his church an ultimatum: "Pay me or I quit the choir!" The church declined his offer and he quit.

The choir suffered his loss for a while, but soon enough someone came along to take his place. Not one of us is indispensable; the church rolls on. But that man has sulked for twenty-three years. He doesn't attend church regularly; when he does, he sits in the congregation with bitterness written all over his face.

He is mad most of the time; he is cynical and critical of the church, especially the music program. But people long ago stopped listening to him. Here is a man who has wasted his talent and who has wasted twenty-three years. Think of what he has missed while making himself miserable through pettiness. Life is too short for littleness, and pettiness is a waste of time, talent, and energy.

I'm thinking of a woman who quite suddenly quit the church. When the pastor asked her why, she said, "My sister passed away on September 20, and I didn't get a sympathy card from my Sunday school class until September 25. I will never forgive the church or my Sunday school class for slighting me like that!"

I wonder what Jesus would say to her. I wonder what the apostle Paul would say, or Phillips Brooks or Mother Teresa. My guess would be that they would say, "Come on now. Life is too short for that." Life is too short for littleness, and pettiness is a waste of time and energy.

I'm thinking of a couple who became upset with their church back in the early 1960s because of a social decision the church made. The couple became sick with bitterness and hostility. It was all they could talk about. At every meal, they fussed at the church. Each evening in the den, they harshly criticized the church and its leaders. They wrote hot letters, looked constantly for materials to use against the church, and made abusive speeches. This went on for five years, and their children looked on and listened and took it all in.

Finally, their hostility spent, the couple decided to come back to the church. But they ran into something they had not counted on—their children didn't want to have anything to do with the church now, and strangely that couple couldn't understand why.

For five years they had denounced the church in front of their children because of one decision made by the administrative board, and inadvertently they had taught their children to hate the church and its people.

Five years of bitterness, five years of pettiness; how do you undo that? How do you correct it? Is it too late? Life is too short for littleness. Pettiness is dangerous, a waste of time and energy, and sometimes a waste of young lives.

+++

CHAPTER 50

THE SIGNS OF DEATH ... AND LIFE

JOHN 1:1-10

Some time ago, an excellent article written by my good friend Bill Hull came to my desk. It is entitled "When Are You Really Dead?" In it, Dr. Hull, in his typically thoughtful way, examines the legal, medical, and moral question of when a person should be considered dead.

As I read Dr. Hull's words, my mind darted back to an experience I had shared some years ago with a good friend. Gladys was her name. She was seventy-two years old. We stood side by side in a small hospital room in the intensive care unit.

As we looked at the silent and still figure of her husband on the hospital bed, she reached over and took my hand. Tears misted our eyes as we looked at the emaciated body of this man with whom she had shared a very special love for more than fifty years.

He was in a coma. He had been in the hospital for months and unable to communicate for several weeks. Now he was hooked up to all kinds of medical machines that were keeping him alive. One was helping him breathe, another was keeping his heart going, and still another was feeding him.

Suddenly Gladys broke the silence. "That's not really Walter," she said. "That's just the old worn-out body that housed his wonderful spirit. They're keeping the vital things going, as I suppose they must. But I've already given him up. I've already said goodbye. I've already released him. I decided several days ago that those machines are working, but really . . . Walter is gone!"

Well, what do you think? Was Gladys right? Was Walter, as she put it, already gone?

When is a person considered to be dead? What is the thin line that distinguishes life and death? What are the signs? When the heart stops? When the brainwaves cease? When there is no breath?

Are the definitions of physical death related in any way to the symptoms of spiritual death? Now that is something to think about, isn't it?

Over the years, the three major evidences of death have been the following: First, no heartbeat. Second, no brain activity. And third, no breath.

Dr. Hull suggests a fourth, namely: "when the machines or other external devices are required to sustain life artificially."

With this as a backdrop, I want to suggest that these four symptoms . . .

✦ no life apart from external machines,
✦ no heartbeat,

✦ no brain activity,

✦ and no breath . . .

are also the precise symptoms of spiritual death. That is, when your faith is fully dependent on somebody else or on the external machines of religion; when your faith loses its heartbeat of concern for others; when your faith stops growing and stretching your brain and challenging your mind; or when your faith loses the spirit-breath of God—then you are in big trouble. You are spiritually dead!

The good news of our Christian faith, however, is resurrection! You can come alive again. God can reawaken the vital signs of life within you.

So, let's take a look at these four signs of death in the hope that, as we do, we might find what makes for abundant life.

FIRST, THOSE WHO HAVE "NO LIFE APART FROM EXTERNAL MACHINES." These people never think for themselves. They never much feel anything. They don't do anything creative. They are religious parasites. They don't give anything. They only draw from others. They have no inner strength, no inner poise, no personal commitment, no philosophy of life, no private celebration of God's presence. If you "pull the plug," their faith will quickly die because there is no inner vitality.

Please don't misunderstand me. We all need help from others. We need good churches to train and inspire us. We need mothers and fathers to show us the way. We need good leaders to challenge us. We need external symbols, liturgies, and rituals. We need a community of faith to encourage and comfort us.

But we also need our own personal faith. We also need our unique encounter with the living Lord. We need a faith within—an inner faith that can sustain us—even if the plug is pulled.

SECOND, THOSE WHOSE FAITH HAS "NO HEART-BEAT." They have no compassion, no concern for others, no sense of mission or service, no love. They think only of themselves. Perhaps knocked about by the problems of life and the troubles of the world, they have become cynical, calloused, critical, cold, and calculating. They don't want to be their brother's keeper. They don't even want to be their brother's brother.

THIRD, THOSE WHOSE "FAITH BRAINWAVES" HAVE STOPPED. No brain activity here. These are the people who stop growing, stretching, thinking, and learning.

A disciple is by definition a "learner," but sometimes people forget that and they close their minds. Closed-mindedness is indeed a sign of spiritual death.

FOURTH, THOSE WHO HAVE "NO BREATH." Remember that in the Scriptures, "breath" is the symbol for the spirit of God. Let me ask if anyone has ever seen or felt the Spirit of God in you. I just wonder if anyone anywhere has ever looked at you or me and somehow caught a glimpse of God's spirit in us. If not, we may be spiritual corpses.

How is it with you? If you were to have a spiritual checkup today, how would you stack up?

✦ Could you make it apart from the external machinery of religion?

✦ Do you have a healthy, loving heartbeat?

✦ Do you have active brainwaves?

✦ Do you have in you the breath of God?

Discussion Guide
for

John D. Schroeder

Chapter 1
Go Out Singing

1. What does God's use of unlikely people tell us about God?
2. Give some biblical examples of God using unlikely people to do great things.
3. Create two lists of likely and unlikely people to be used by God. Why are the likely often passed by?
4. What qualities might unlikely people possess that make them valuable to God?

Chapter 2
If You Get Where You Are Going, Where Will You Be?

1. Share a time when you ended up in the wrong place.
2. Name some signs of being on the right path.

3. Why are good intentions not enough?

4. What causes people to get lost or off course?

Chapter 3
Is It Sinful to Get Angry?

1. Share a time when you got angry and regretted it.

2. Give an example of adolescent anger.

3. Why is seething anger so dangerous?

4. Reflect on / discuss righteous indignation and how Jesus modeled this behavior.

Chapter 4
When Your Heart Is Broken

1. Describe some of the ways hearts get broken.

2. How can church fellowship help you fight sorrow?

3. Share a time when you gained power and healing by helping others.

4. How can the presence of God help you? What do you need to do to get help from God?

Chapter 5
Should I Forgive?

1. Why is forgiveness such a struggle for us?

2. Name some benefits of being a forgiving person.

3. Share a time when you struggled with forgiveness.

4. What did Jesus teach about forgiveness? How did he model this behavior?

Chapter 6
When It's Hard to Believe

1. Describe some times in life when maintaining your faith is a struggle.

2. Name some of the ways our beliefs may be challenged.

3. How does faith get strengthened?

4. When it is hard to believe, what should you do?

Chapter 7
Talking a Good Game Is Not Enough

1. Why do people often fail to turn talk into action?

2. How do creeds become deeds?

3. Reflect on / discuss what it means that faith is a lifestyle.

4. Name some of the costs of practicing what we preach.

Chapter 8
You Have to Finish What You Start

1. Give some reasons you should finish what you start.

2. Why are tasks often left unfinished?

3. What needs to happen in order to reach a goal?

4. Share something you want to accomplish.

Chapter 9
A Bad Case of the Simples

1. Share a time when you realized something was not as simple as you first thought.
2. Reflect on / discuss the dangers of oversimplification.
3. What did you learn about practice and patience from this chapter?
4. How do you develop commitment to see things through?

Chapter 10
Roadblocks

1. What can we learn from Paul about roadblocks?
2. Name some common roadblocks in life.
3. Share a time when you experienced a closed road.
4. How should we respond to roadblocks? List some strategies.

Chapter 11
Some Things Are Worth Saying Over and Over

1. Why is true wisdom worth repeating?
2. Reflect on / discuss the importance of people.
3. Why is discipleship costly?
4. Describe the traits and behavior of God as our loving Father.

Chapter 12
The Choice Is Yours: You Can Build Up or Tear Down

1. Share a time when you faced a choice to build up or tear down.
2. How can encouragement change lives?
3. Why is laughter and humor needed each day?
4. Reflect on / discuss why people punish instead of offering pardon.

Chapter 13
The Measuring Stick Is Love

1. How has your "religion" changed over the years?
2. Reflect on / discuss a moment when you realized the importance of love.
3. How and why does narrow religion fail us?
4. Reflect on / discuss ways in which love can be used as a measuring stick.

Chapter 14
Are You Building Bridges or Walls?

1. Name some of the reasons people build walls.
2. Is it harder to build a wall or a bridge? Explain.
3. Why are bridges better than walls?
4. What kind of bridges need to be built today?

Chapter 15
Truly, This Man Was God's Son!

1. What does the cross tell us about love?
2. Reflect on / discuss the importance of humility.
3. How did Jesus model forgiveness?
4. What lessons can we learn from Jesus on the cross?

Chapter 16
Are You Trapped by Your Fears?

1. Share a time when you were trapped in a prison of your own making.
2. Describe some of the fears that trap us. Which are the worst?
3. Why is fear so dangerous?
4. Reflect on / discuss ways to break free from fear.

Chapter 17
This Is My Moment

1. Name some of the crucial moments in life.
2. What often causes us to miss important moments?
3. Briefly reflect on / discuss each of the six missed moments listed in this chapter.
4. What qualities does it take to seize great moments in life?

Chapter 18
Resilience: The Strength to Bend without Breaking

1. Share a time when you were resilient.
2. What is meant by resilience? Give some qualities and characteristics of resilience.
3. How can we all become more resilient?
4. Reflect on / discuss the four areas where all of us could use more resilience.

Chapter 19
When Trouble Comes

1. How do you normally respond when trouble comes your way?
2. What choices do we have when faced with trouble?
3. Reflect on / discuss how Jesus responded to the troubles he encountered.
4. How can our troubles make us better people?

Chapter 20
The Truth Will Set You Free

1. What often prevents us from seeing the truth?
2. Name some things in life that lock us up.
3. How does it feel to be free?
4. What do we need to do to be set free by the truth of Christ?

Chapter 21
Why Not You?

1. Reflect on / discuss why the question "Why not you?" is so powerful and applies to all of us.
2. Give some reasons we wait for others to act instead of responding ourselves.
3. When you see a problem, what should you do?
4. What expectations does God have about our solving problems?

Chapter 22
Keep on Keeping On

1. Share a time when you struggled with disillusionment.
2. List some of the painful moments in life.
3. Reflect on / discuss how loving others can help you in tough times.
4. Why is it important to trust and worship God during life's difficulties?

Chapter 23
When Crisis Comes

1. Why is it important to prepare for a crisis?
2. How does being familiar with the Bible help you in a crisis?
3. Reflect on / discuss how you develop a strong prayer life.
4. Share what helps you most in a crisis.

Chapter 24
The Power of Words

1. Reflect on / discuss why words are important and powerful.
2. How are kindness and faith connected?
3. Name some words of appreciation that lift people up.
4. Reflect on / discuss the power of words of love.

Chapter 25
Spiritual Cataracts

1. Reflect on / discuss what is meant by spiritual cataracts.
2. What's the connection between your viewpoint and your spiritual life?
3. Share a time when you did not see things clearly.
4. How can we avoid spiritual cataracts?

Chapter 26
Cut it Off—Throw It Away? Did Jesus Really Mean That?

1. What was the symbolic message of Jesus in his Sermon on the Mount?
2. Reflect on / discuss the times in life when we need to cut off and get rid of problems.
3. Name some of the spiritual poisons that need to be cut out and removed.
4. Why do we all need radical surgery at some point in our lives?

Chapter 27
One Step at a Time

1. Reflect on / discuss the wisdom of taking one step at a time.

2. Share an experience when you discovered the importance of taking single steps.

3. What are some keys to taking slow and deliberate steps?

4. Reflect on / discuss how we see the principle of "one step at a time" in the life of Jesus.

Chapter 28
Are You Really Committed?

1. Reflect on / discuss the importance of making commitments.

2. Why are people reluctant to make commitments?

3. Name some keys to remaining committed.

4. Give some examples of commitment as found in the Bible.

Chapter 29
The Power of Your Influence

1. Name some people who have influenced your life.

2. Reflect on / discuss the ways that we influence others.

3. Why is it important to strive to be a good example? How can we be a good influence?

4. How can we live a Christ-inspired life?

Chapter 30
Made for the Skies and Crammed in a Cage

1. Share a time when you felt as if you were caged.

2. Name some common causes of confinement.

3. How can we escape from our cages? Reflect on / discuss some strategies.

4. Reflect on / discuss how God can help you achieve your full potential.

Chapter 31
I Distinctly Remember Forgetting That!

1. Why do we need to purposely forget some things?

2. Name some keys to being able to forget.

3. What obstacles can make it difficult to forget?

4. Why is it often wise to forget past accomplishments?

Chapter 32
The Power of Love

1. Why is love the most important thing in the world?

2. Share a time when you experienced the power of love.

3. How do we learn to love and be better lovers?

4. Compare the benefits and risks of loving others.

Chapter 33
The Dangers of Success

1. Name some common dangers of success.
2. Has a success ever hurt you? Explain.
3. Why are we often tempted to rest on our laurels?
4. How can we avoid some of the dangers that can come with success?

Chapter 34
Change Your Attitudes and Change Your Life

1. Why is attitude so important in life?
2. Reflect on / discuss how and why life is determined by our attitude.
3. List some strategies for attitude change.
4. Explain why your destiny is a matter of choice, not chance.

Chapter 35
The Beauty of Uniqueness—or It's OK to Be Different

1. Name something that is unique about you.
2. How is being different a blessing?
3. Why do we need to be tolerant of differences in others?
4. Reflect on / discuss how and why our individual pathways to God are different.

Chapter 36
Friendship with God

1. Name some benefits of friendship with God.
2. Reflect on / discuss the four basic elements of friendship. How are they related to friendship with God?
3. Share some ideas on how we can become better friends with God.
4. What kind of friendship do you want with God?

Chapter 37
Our Father

1. Reflect on / discuss the story of Paul Hawks. What impresses you about it?
2. What is so significant about the two words Our Father?
3. How can the words Our Father change us?
4. Reflect on / discuss how these words help us realize our true identity and our relationship with others.

Chapter 38
The Parable of the Locksmith

1. Reflect on / discuss what we can learn from this parable.
2. Name some of the ways people are enslaved or imprisoned.
3. Once Christ unlocks our prison door, what does he want us to do?
4. Reflect on / discuss the connection between the parable of the locksmith and the prayer of Saint Francis of Assisi.

Chapter 39
There Are No Respectable Excuses for Not Loving

1. Which of the four excuses listed do you think is most common, and why?
2. What causes us to make these excuses?
3. How are others affected by our lack of love?
4. What can you do when you are tempted to make an excuse instead of showing genuine love?

Chapter 40
Jesus, the Message and the Messenger

1. Reflect on / discuss how Jesus was both the Message and the Messenger.
2. How and why has trust become our problem?
3. Reflect on / discuss how God has shown us he means what he says.
4. How should we respond to the Message and the Messenger?

Chapter 41
Who's in Control?

1. Reflect on / discuss why many people lack control of their own lives.
2. List some of the symptoms of a lack of control.
3. How do people become controlled by others? How do people become controlled by circumstances?

4. Reflect on / discuss ways we can give God more control over our lives. What needs to be done? What are some first steps?

Chapter 42
What Can One Person Do?

1. Reflect on / discuss the parable in this chapter and the lessons we can learn from it.
2. What makes us feel insignificant?
3. Why are we, in reality, very significant and powerful?
4. What can one person do?

Chapter 43
Is Your Faith Too Small?

1. Why can faith remain small and fail to grow?
2. Share a time when you wished for more faith.
3. Describe the dangers of having a faith too small.
4. How can we grow our faith and make it more powerful?

Chapter 44
Tell Me, Please, How to Be Happy

1. Reflect on / discuss what makes happiness so elusive.
2. How much of happiness is attitude?
3. Explain why God is the lasting and true source of happiness.
4. What are healthy and productive methods of coping with unhappiness?

Chapter 45
The Dangers of Overreacting

1. Share a time when you overreacted or were tempted to act impulsively.
2. List some of the virtues of patience.
3. Reflect on / discuss the dangers of overreacting.
4. How do you distinguish between acting and overreacting?

Chapter 46
What Does It Mean to Be a Christian?

1. List some words that would describe Christian behavior.
2. Reflect on / discuss the four ways a Christian sees through the eyes of Christ.
3. Name some ways we can be a "little Christ."
4. Why do you think the rich young ruler failed to respond and follow Jesus?

Chapter 47
Snatching Defeat from the Jaws of Victory

1. Reflect on / discuss the dangers of early success.
2. Why do people give in and desire to quit?
3. Name some keys to winning at life and living victoriously.
4. When we struggle to move forward, what should we try to remember?

Chapter 48
What Are the Questions?

1. Reflect on / discuss why the five questions in this chapter are important and need answers.
2. How can asking questions help us in life?
3. Reflect on / discuss how to get answers to important questions. How do you begin?
4. What is meant by "Christ is the answer"?

Chapter 49
Life Is Much Too Short for Pettiness

1. Reflect on / discuss why pettiness is a spiritual cancer.
2. How does it feel to be on the receiving end of pettiness?
3. Name some sources or causes of pettiness.
4. List some ways to avoid pettiness.

Chapter 50
The Signs of Death . . . and Life

1. How are the definitions of physical death related to the symptoms of spiritual death?
2. Name some signs of abundant life.
3. Reflect on / discuss the four warning signs of spiritual death.
4. What is a spiritual checkup? When is it needed?